Real Ghost Stories

Sightings, Ouija Board Messages and Séances

CRAIG HAMILTON-PARKER

DEDICATION

For all those who had the courage
to share their strange stories with us

CONTENTS

ACKNOWLEDGMENTS

Many thanks to my editors and journalist friends
who followed up many of these stories
to verify their authenticity.

1 INTRODUCTION

For over thirty years, I have written paranormal columns for the national British newspapers and for international magazines and publications. Readers were invited to mail me their true stories, questions, and experiences, and I would answer through my columns. Often the letters sent were very long and detailed, but for clarity and space I had to abridge them considerably. They were then scrutinised by the subeditor, and in many instances the sender was telephoned so that we could check the factual details and accuracy of my column. This journalistic methodology, I believe, has helped make these stories easy to read, properly verified, and completely authentic.

I was writing my first columns in the days before the Internet, so, unlike many of today's books of this kind, the accounts are unique and have not been unscrupulously scrapped from unreliable forums, throw-away Twitter feeds, and crazy blogs and websites. These stories are real accounts that have been verified by my qualified journalist colleagues.

Over the years, I have written for many different publications targeted at different age groups, genders, and income groups. There are a lot of stories here from

Scotland and Ireland, as my columns in these countries generated some of the most interesting letters. This could be something to do with the old Irish spiritual traditions and the legendary "Highland Seers," or simply because the Celts love a good spooky story! In the mix are also tales from my columns in England, America, Australia, and South Africa, and a few from a Latvian newspaper column that I wrote for a short time.

One of my most long-standing columns was for a newspaper targeted at the older generation, so you will read here a few paranormal accounts from people living at the time of the Second World War. I personally found these particularly interesting, as they come from a time when talk about ghosts and spirits was often dismissed as nonsense or seen as a taboo topic. For some of my readers, it took courage to write to me and see their story published.

I have been working as a spiritualist medium for most of my life, and for the first part of my spiritual career I kept it a secret that I was mediumistic, as many people would throw scorn or be offended by the idea. Now every Tom, Dick, and Harry claims to be a psychic or medium because of the culture of trashy TV ghost hunts, spooky video games, and movies like Harry Potter, which have made the whole topic cool and fashionable. The problem is that it is hard to sort the true medium from the self-deluded phonies, and similarly it is hard to sort the real ghost stories from the fantasy and fakes.

I hope that my many years of experience as a professional medium and the scrutiny and care that have gone into verifying these accounts will go some way toward helping to dispel some of the myths and misconceptions that surround this topic, and also will inspire you to look more deeply into the fascinating world of the paranormal.

2 GHOST SIGHTINGS

TAKE THE GHOST TRAIN

The strangest experience of my life happened when my wife and I were staying in Colombo, Sri Lanka. The Tamil Tiger terrorists were active at the time, and we were advised by our hotelier not to go out after curfew and to avoid the beach in particular. But one night we had a problem getting back, and in order to avoid the beach, we had to take a route along the railway line.

The old steam trains normally made quite a racket. You could hear them hissing and clanking from miles away. I noticed a bright light behind us. Assuming that a train was coming, I quickly pulled my wife away from the rails as a large train brushed by, almost touching us.

Even though it was an old steam train, it was totally silent—not quiet, but *totally* silent. The steam, the wheels, and the carriages made not a single sound. We were so close that we could also see that the train had no driver, no passengers, and no guard.

I'm a sceptical man—I was trained in the Navy and have worked as a councillor—so I went next morning to ask the stationmaster about the incident. He insisted that no trains passed that way at the times I said. And he added that the track where we had walked had been the site of a number of fatal train disasters!

Did we see a ghost train? My wife thinks that if we had stayed put, it would have passed right through us. What do you think?

—John & Elsie S.

You certainty wouldn't be the first to see a ghost train. One of the most famous has been seen by hundreds of people in Illinois in America. When President Abraham Lincoln (who openly held séances in the White House) died in 1856, his body was transported for burial on a special funeral train. Now, every year on the anniversary, his ghost train is seen slowly driving down the tracks. It is said to be manned by skeletons, with an entourage of blue-coated men walking behind.

SPIRIT IN THE SOFA

When I was in my twenties, I shared a local flat with a student. Although the place was comfortable and well decorated, it was the weirdest place I have ever lived in. It all started when a large oval mirror began moving by itself. Whenever I relaxed or let my mind drift, a loud crackling sound would be heard and sometimes the sound of rustling papers. If we moved towards the noise, it would stop immediately. The disturbances became so frequent that it was difficult to sleep at night!

Early one evening, we were relaxing in the lounge. The student was lying on the floor, writing an essay. Suddenly I was aware that someone else was with us. I saw the white figure of a woman, standing in the corner of the room. My eyes must have been like saucers, but I felt no fear. To this day, I vividly remember what she was wearing and how she seemed to shine. But the strangest thing of all was that where she stood was an armchair. She was standing right through it!

—Linda H.

You are very psychic. The occurrences appear to happen whenever you are in a state of deep relaxation. You may have experienced a light trance state of mind, and your psychic energies were engaged to build a bridge between the worlds. I am aware that you also have premonitions that come true, and that on one occasion your life was saved because of a guiding voice. Train your gifts properly, and you could become an excellent medium.

I SAW A FACELESS AIRMAN

I'm sure that the old, oak-beamed house that I used to rent rooms at is haunted. One night I saw, standing in front of me, the ghostly figure of man dressed in an airman's uniform from the Second World War. It was so clear: he wore a short brown bomber jacket, a flat cap, and light trousers, but his collar was turned up, so that I couldn't see his face. I screamed out in terror.

The landlady knew the ghost. It was her husband, who had died eighteen months before. He had been an airman and continued to wear a brown bomber jacket throughout his life. At the end, he suffered from leukaemia. This made him feel the cold, so he would always wear his collar turned up. It obscured much of his face.

—Michelle S.

Although the ghost frightened you, your experience must have brought comfort to your landlady. The detail of his visual communication provides enough proof to indicate to her that her loved one survived bodily death—which, of course, we all do. Your terror was her comfort.

BEWARE OF THE GHOST

When I was a postman, I had to deliver to a new block of flats, which had been built for the elderly. I had been doing this for about four years without any problems. One morning I was delivering as usual, when on the third flight of stairs I had a very strong feeling that someone was behind me. I turned around, but nobody was there. The feeling got worse as I approached the flat door. I'm a level-headed bloke, but I was beginning to get very scared. Suddenly I felt something cold touch my neck. I hastily delivered the letters and was nearly running as I left the premises.

The next morning, at the same flat, with the experience fresh in my mind, I delivered some more letters. A neighbour opened her door. "I wouldn't bother if I were you," she said. "The lady in that flat died a few days ago." Now I knew that what happened wasn't a figment of my imagination.

—Neil H.

You experienced *clairsentience*, which is the mediumistic ability to sense the presence of spirits. When you "see" a spirit communicator, it is called *clairvoyance*, and when you "hear" their voice, it is called *clairaudience*. Most mediumship is a combination of the three. I am aware that you have also seen the spirit of your father. With your psychic abilities, you could one day perhaps deliver messages from people in the afterlife.

I SPOOKED THE SPOOK

When I moved into my new home, which is built on an old air base, I looked at the front room and thought, "This room should be blue." Then, one evening while quietly watching television, I saw the room change in front of my eyes. Everything was suddenly blue, then instantly reverted back to normality.

A few days later, I walked into the same room and saw the figure of a large man standing in the middle of the room. We walked towards each other, and he passed straight through me. I screamed out: "I live here now! You don't. Go away!"

I haven't had any more strange phenomena happen. I think that we must have frightened each other so much that the ghost hasn't dared come back.

—Carol P.

Sightings of ghosts have been reported at most of the WW2 airbases. Some mediums will clear haunted places by helping the earth-bound spirits to realise that they are dead and encourage them to move into the spirit world. It sounds like you instinctively did this, but I pity the poor ghost who had such a sudden awakening.

A GHOST PINNED ME TO THE BED

I was asked by a friend to "dog sit" over the weekend. I must admit, I have never felt at ease in her house. It was old, large, and a little spooky, but there was something else about it—it had an eerie feeling that I couldn't quite put my finger on.

I went to bed with a good book and eventually drifted off to sleep. Some hours later, I awoke unable to breath and choking—it was as if somebody was sitting on my chest! There was an immense weight pinning me to the bed. I thought I was dying by having the breath squeezed out of my body. Somehow

I managed to throw myself out of bed and staggered downstairs, gulping in air as I went.

I never slept there again. My unwelcome nocturnal visitor obviously objected to my presence. And I can take a hint!

—Di S.

There's a part of the brain at the back of the head that inhibits body movement when we sleep. If it didn't, we would act out our dreams and thrash wildly around in bed. Many people experience "sleep paralysis" when the conscious mind wakes up before this restraining function does. The result is a feeling of immobility and suffocation. Did your restlessness trigger sleep paralysis, or were paranormal forces at work? We'll never know for certain.

MURDERED FREDDIE RETURNS FROM THE GRAVE

We live in a traditional farmhouse, which was probably built with ancient stone from a nearby ruin. We have a pillar on each side of the sitting room fireplace. Legend has it that two brothers once lived here and jointly inherited it. They had an argument, and one murdered the other.

We now occasionally have spooky occurrences. One of the bedroom doors sometimes opens, and we hear footsteps walk along the landing and down the stairs. At the end of this journey, the stair door opens.

But we're not afraid of the ghost. Every time it happens, we say, "Oh, Fred, we do wish you'd learn to shut the door."

We have four adult children. The two girls are now married, and only one of our sons now lives at home. We have all experienced "Fred," and it is my son's bedroom door that opens. He is not bothered by it at all. Even our three dogs and three cats do not react to friendly "Fred."

—Mrs. Jane F.

Fred would probably scare the pants off most people. But I believe that you take the right attitude. Ghosts can't hurt you, so why be frightened of them? Do any other readers have a friendly (or otherwise) resident spook?

GHOST GIVES ME SLEEPLESS NIGHTS

I am terrified at night, as I believe that I am being menaced by a ghost or spirit. If I awake during the night, I see what I would call "smoke" in my room. At first, I would jump out of bed, thinking that the house was on fire, but now I realise it is nothing to do with this world. If I approach it, it just disappears.

One night, I saw the harrowing sight of my bedclothes being slowly pulled off the bed. But the last straw was when I felt "it" move to the side of the bed and poke me hard in the arm. I prayed out loud, but it wouldn't go away.

I'm frightened to go to sleep. What can I do?

—Alma W.

Your biggest enemy is your own fear. First you have to be strong with yourself and not give in to fear. Secondly you have to be realistic and make sure that the fog is not caused by an eye problem. If you decide that you really do have a negative spirit, I suggest that you say, "Clear off!" and then just ignore it. These things prey on fear, and if you refuse to be ruffled, it will eventually give up pestering you. Okay, it frightens you, but it cannot physically hurt you. If all else fails, call your local spiritualists, who may be able to recommend a local medium to help get rid of it.

HORROR AT THE HAUNTED BOAT

When I was a crew member aboard the Bristol-registered ship *Castle Combe*, we went to a small quarrying creek on the Welsh coast. It was one of those places where the ebbing tide left the ship high and dry. My attention was drawn to a dilapidated vessel anchored a little distance out. It looked like it was ready for the breaker's yard. One night, I saw a faint light coming from one of the portholes so decided to walk over to it and have a look.

As I climbed aboard the deserted ship, I felt unease. I opened the door to the crew's cabins and was confronted by a man. He wore a mustard-coloured coat with a cloth cap pulled over his eyes. But he was floating three feet above the ground! I dashed back to my own ship.

The next day, I was worried by what I had seen. Had someone, perhaps, hung themselves? I had to go back and find out. I opened the same door again and in the daylight could see a large number of glass containers. "Of course, that was the answer," I consoled myself. The man must have been standing on one of them, which I couldn't see in the darkness!

—Jim J.

I absolutely love spooky stories about the sea. Have any more of our seafarers a strange tale to tell? Write to the usual address and let us know.

GHOST GIVES REASSURANCE

It was one of those times when everything that could go wrong did go wrong. To top it all, my cat died of kidney failure. In despair, I sat on my settee at home, put my head in my hands, and had a good cry.

I stopped when I felt a hand gently squeeze my shoulder. Looking up, I saw my dead ex-husband. He was as clear as day and looked just as he did when we first met, with his trilby hat cocked to one side. When I looked again, he was gone.

Do you think that he was trying to reassure me in my moment of grief?
—Melinda D.

Even though you divorced, there must still have been some love between you both. Maybe when the day comes and you meet in the afterlife, you will resolve the difficulties that you had in life and share love once more? I'm sure that reassurance was being given to you.

DID A GHOST SHARE MY BED?

I am seventy-six years old and not subject to fantasy, but one night, when I was staying at a friend's house, a strange thing happened. As I lay in bed, the figure of a woman, dressed in long, mustard-coloured robes, floated into my room. She floated by the side of the bed and then lay down beside me! She spoke to me, but her words were indistinct. I asked her to repeat the words but still couldn't make them out. Then she just faded away. In the morning, I asked my friends if anyone had entered my room that night, and of course they hadn't. Sometimes I do have very vivid dreams, but throughout this experience I was fully awake.
—Elizabeth D.

Maybe a ghost did share your bed but there is another possible explanation. Some people , particularly those who are capable of vivid dreams, can enter a state of awareness known as lucid dreaming. The dreamer "wakes up" within the dream and retains the same clarity of thinking, as in normal waking consciousness.

Research now reveals that these lucid dreamers can direct their dreams, much like a film director directs a film, and can even alter the dream's content at will.

A technique known as "Creative Sleep," based on methods used by Tibetan Yogis over four centuries ago, teaches the subject to solve problems and gain access to hidden stores of energy. Lucid dreaming can also open our awareness to the spirit world.

THIS GHOST WON'T LEAVE US ALONE

I arranged for a medium to visit our house because we were troubled by a ghost. While the medium was with us, the rug in the living room lifted up, and there was a very loud thumping on the floor, as if it was being hit by a stick. The medium's advice was to be strong and firmly tell the entity to go away. I've had other mediums visit as well, but the problems persisted.

Before the spirit activity, a sweet, sickly smell fills the whole house. I experience a numbness and coldness, as if being touched by something.

Often things will fall by themselves, and on one occasion the ironing board nearly hit my young daughter. Also, writing appears on my windows, and no matter how hard I scrub, it will not disappear. It couldn't be my daughter doing this, as she can't write yet, and I am careful to keep pens out of reach. The strange smell started again when I decided to write to you today. What should I do?
—Theresa S.

We've smelled the same sweet sickly smell that occurs when an earth-bound spirit makes itself known. The spirit presence is strong, so your best option would be to ask your medium friends if they can work together.

A group of mediums will be able to make a strong challenge. They would find out the spirit's identity and convince it to go on to the spirit world. The advice given to you to be strong and firm with the entity is wise.

SPOOKY MONK

At about 4:00 in the morning, I was awoken from a deep sleep by a strong feeling that there was somebody in my bedroom. I felt that I was being watched. The room was cold. Slowly I turned my head and saw the shadowy form of a monk standing beside my bed. He was standing with his head bowed and arms folded at waist level. Inside the hood, there was just darkness. As I sat up, the figure faded away.

I have no idea what this was all about but am sure that I didn't imagine any of this. Can you explain it?
—Terry F.

I wish that I could explain this one adequately, as so many people write to say that they've seen the same thing. We live on a site that was once a monastery. My wife tells me that the ghost of a monk appeared in our living room in front of her sceptical brother, who was pooh-poohing our work. He was so scared by what he saw that he went to church every day for a week afterwards. Many mediums believe that monks and nuns continue their spiritual work in the afterlife as guardians of the living.

THINGS THAT GO BUMP IN THE BEDROOM

I could sense there was someone in the room watching me. The next thing I knew, the bed sank, as if someone had sat down on it. I was too scared to look at it. I have also had pictures falling off the wall for no apparent reason. Please could you tell me what all this means?

Also, I was in my bed, drifting off to sleep, when I felt the presence of someone sitting on the bed. The bed actually went down. I heard a voice that told me not to be afraid, as they just wanted to hold my hand and be with me. A coldness went up my arm.

—Helen S.

Now you have something in common with Sarah Lancashire, who plays the buxom barmaid Raquel in *Coronation Street*. She was also shocked to see a ghost in her bedroom. Her Manchester bedroom rattled with the ghost of a Victorian woman carrying her screaming baby. She said: "It stared into my eyes and raised a withered hand, as if trying to speak to me, but then vanished. I have two young sons of my own, but I have never heard sounds like that baby screaming."

GHOST OF MINER SAVED MY FRIEND

I was always ridiculed by my friends and work mates because I believe that the dead can contact the living. Nobody would ever believe me. But they changed their tune late one night, when the siren blared and news arrived from the coal pit.

My friend had been working deep in the pit, when he saw the ghostly shape of another miner approach him. Shocked, my friend jumped up from where he was working and followed the phantom down the passage. As soon as he got close, the figure faded away into thin air.

As he turned around to return to his workplace, the ceiling of the tunnel behind him collapsed with a crash. If he hadn't followed the spectre, he would have died in the accident. The ghost had saved his life.

—Mr. G. M.

This is not the first report of a haunted mine. As reported in the *Cambrian News* on November 14, 1986, a journalist claims that at the old mine workings he saw "a white or pale-blue shape, about the size of a small man. It gave off a sort of glow, but not like a torch." The reporter heard later that lights had occasionally been seen emerging from the mine at night and moving off slowly into the sky.

A LITTLE TERROR

A fire killed the previous occupant of our house. He died drunk in the kitchen. We have experienced some odd happenings: pictures fall, ornaments move, there was an onion in the frying pan, a cornflake packet in the fringe, all the cutlery was in the sink, and the ice-cube maker was in the bin. Sometimes at night I hear sounds, as if someone is gasping for breath. I have a three-year-old child and worry if these things may be dangerous.
—Claire D.

Are you sure your three-year-old hasn't been up to no good? I heard breathing one night only to discover that a window was left open, and the curtain was rubbing on the windowsill.

JAGGER GETS THE JITTERS

I went on a residential course to Stansted Hall, the headquarters of Spiritualism, to make a study of mediumship. Stansted is a very old manor house that has been used for thousands of séances.

On the second night of my stay, I felt a presence in my room. I looked towards the bay window and clearly saw the figure of a monk, dressed in brown robes and a hood. I was terrified because it was so very real.

At afternoon tea the next day, a lady started talking about her experience that same night. To my shock, she said that she had seen, while strolling in the grounds, a monk staring from one of the windows.

"Which window?" I exclaimed. She took me outside to show me. It was my room!

—Marion L.

This figure has been seen before. The late president of Spiritualism, Gordon Higginson, spoke to a monk in the Hall's library. After the man left, Gordon asked at reception who the monk was, but was told that nobody had entered or left the room.

Some celebrities have had similar experiences. For example, in November 1990, singer Mick Jagger was frightened off buying a Gothic mansion by a bell-ringing, eighteenth-century ghost. Anna-Maria Sliwinski, the housekeeper of Donnington Grove House in Newbury, said of it: "I have heard the ghost first-hand. I heard strange chimes on a windless night. The bells were ringing in the tower, but there was nobody else in the house."

NEIGHBOUR PROVES THAT GHOST IS REAL

It was late at night when I saw a ghost appear in the living room of our new house. An old lady stood with her back to me and was leaning on the mantelpiece. She had long, snow-white hair, was stooped badly, and held a walking stick in her right hand. I heard the name "Port." The lady didn't resemble any-one I had known before, but all was explained when I mentioned her to our neighbours. "A Mrs. Port lived in your house years ago," she said, turning white with fright. "She had very long, white hair, and her back was bent."

Could this all be in my mind, or did I really see a ghost?

—D. W.

It sounds real to us. It's true that some ghosts are just fantasy, but you were able to prove concrete facts about your phantom friend. She won't do you any harm. She probably still takes an interest in her old house and came to have a look at you.

MY HAUNTED CAR

It's not my house that's haunted but my car. When I'm driving alone, I have the overwhelming sensation that someone is sitting next to me in the passenger seat. On one occasion, the seatbelt warning light stayed on, even though my own belt was secured. Do you think that my car is really haunted?
—Jenny R.

If you put the seatbelt into the passenger's clip by accident, then the warning light would stay on. Try it and see. This is not the first report we've heard about a haunted car. Villagers of the Long district, in the Phrae province of Thailand, panicked recently when two dozen elderly people died in quick succession. There were strange stories circulating about a ghostly pick-up truck that arrived without a driver. The villagers, to repel the ghost, festooned their homes with banners saying, "This house does not have any old people."

PHOTO PROVES THAT GRAVEYARD GHOST WAS REAL

I was brought up by my grandmother from the age of eighteen months and never knew my mother or father. My father's name was never mentioned.
It wasn't until I was forty-six years old that I discovered his name, and that for all these years he lived only a half-hour's bus ride away from me! Also, I discovered I had two sisters and a half-brother. From the information on the death certificate, I found out

where my father was buried. I went straight to the cemetery.

I knelt down beside my father's neglected grave and sobbed, "Father, if only you'd lived long enough for me to see what you looked like."

When I looked up, I saw the ghostly figure of a man dressed in a blue uniform. He was standing on the top of a grave in a position that would be impossible for a real person to climb to. I also noticed that the figure faded away from below the knee, and there were no feet. He smiled at me.

In utter horror I fled from the graveyard.

When I met my new-found sister, I explained what happened and described the man I saw. She said nothing but handed me a photograph of my father—the first picture I had ever seen of him.

It was the exact likeness of the ghost I had seen in the graveyard.

—Mrs. Jean C., Appleby, Cumbria

The reasons you were abandoned as a baby will remain secret and, hard as it is not knowing, you must emotionally let go of the past. You saw your father's spirit, and the photograph proved to you that the experience was real. A long time hence, when you enter the greater life, your father will explain everything that happened and erase the mystery forever.

TERRORISED BY EMMERDALE GHOST

At my last address, my family and myself were aware that we had a ghost who would only appear between the months of November and March. We called him "Amos" because he seemed to be grumpy, like the character in Emmerdale Farm.

One night in February, we had a power cut for eighteen hours. My wife went with the children round to her mother's house, where it was more comfortable, and I lit some candles and sat at home.

At 8:30 in the evening, one of the neighbours, who had been away, called to ask why there was no power. I invited her in, and she sat in the armchair by the window—the same chair that many of us had felt the ghostly presence in the past.

The woman then seemed to fall into a trance. I saw her features change, and she boomed out in a loud, male voice, "I've got to f—— speak!" Her voice sounded horrible, and the bad language that came from her mouth was appalling.

I must admit I panicked. I jumped up and pulled her from the chair, which brought her immediately to her senses. She was tremendously shaken and had no idea what she'd been saying.

I spent the rest of the night alone and very, very frightened.

—Tony W.

You mention elsewhere in your letter that sometimes, when you've had an argument, the room goes cold, plants stems have snapped, and objects have flown across the room by themselves. This may indicate that you have a rare form of psychic energy that can directly influence the material world. If you could be trained, you would make a first-class medium. The combination of your powers and the woman's trance abilities may have allowed the spirit to manifest. Unfortunately you tell us no more about the woman who visited. Some people with psychiatric disorders will make vulgar outbursts without realising that they've spoken.

3 POLTERGEISTS

POLTERGEIST IN THE ATTIC

When I was seventeen, my brother and I went to stay with a friend for a few days. During the night, when I was alone in the house, I heard loud banging noises coming from the attic bedroom. I was terrified and went outside to check no one was on the roof. But the bangs kept on coming.

The phone rang. It was my brother calling to say that he was worried about me for some inexplicable reason. When I explained my fears, he came straight home and examined the attic room. We found about a dozen books scattered around the room. They could never have fallen from shelves because of the way they were strewn about. Also, the bed's mattress was soaking, but the duvet cover was stone dry.

Do you think that I was similar in age to a ghost, who normally lived quietly on the premises but now wanted to communicate? I had a very unhappy childhood and wonder if that's why a spirit tried to get in touch with me.

—Ms. Colin D.

Although there may be a straightforward explanation for the noises you heard, your experience does have some of the classic signs of poltergeist activity. Most reported accounts of poltergeists centre around adolescents who've had a very unhappy childhood. Disturbances usually—but not always—occur at night, and very many reports describe a wetness left behind after the activity. Poltergeists are not ghosts or conscious entities. They result from psychokinetic energy projected from yourself. Your inner problems expressed themselves by making objects move. It is the same sort of energy that enabled Uri Geller to bend spoons by paranormal means.

THE REAL X FILES AT WARD TWELVE

In 1950 I was stationed at an RAF Hospital at Ely. As duty officer, I was completing a routine night patrol of the building when, to my surprise, I met a nurse. She asked me where Ward Twelve was, and I directed her to the appropriate corridor. As I had never seen this nurse before, I informed the matron, but she had seen no one in the vicinity of Ward Twelve. I was about to leave when the Sister and I became aware of footsteps within the ward itself. Our flashlights revealed nothing. We turned the main lights on and saw no one, but clearly heard the same mysterious footsteps walk past us.

The mystery was never satisfactory solved, although the matron could remember a young nurse who had contracted a fatal disease while working on Ward Twelve. Her description fitted exactly that of the lady I had spoken with that night.

But that was not the end of the matter. Furniture started to wobble and fall over, and then smaller items were seen by myself and others flying around, crashing against walls, and breaking windows. A guard was immediately posted around the area, and a thorough investigation ruled out the obvious, such as pranksters. The Institute for Psychical Research were called to investigate but were unable to pin down the cause of the phenomena. Their instruments measured an unexplained temperature drop in the building, despite the blazing heat of a summer's day outside.

—Hugh S.

The phenomenon that causes objects to move and poltergeist activity is called *psychokinesis*. Many researchers believe that objects are moved by an unknown human energy. In the presence of some people, objects will move, spoons bend, and room temperatures change. Others argue that there are spirit forces at work. Your ghostly encounter may suggest the latter.

I DARE NOT LOOK AT THE PHANTOM'S FACE

This is the first time that I have ever told anyone about my fears, but I am deeply troubled and wonder if you can help. Like many other of your readers, I have had psychic experiences and dreams that have come true.

My most frightening psychic experiences happened when I owned a night club in at Weston-Super-Mare. I would dream, although sometimes it was more like a waking vision, of a woman in a long, black, Victorian dress with a bustle and heavy embroidery on her sleeves. Her face was always turned away from me, and she would be standing by an open fireplace. I "knew" that her face hid something terrible. I dared not look at it.

I assumed it was just a dream, until a lady who worked for us said that she'd seen a ghost that was exactly the same as my dream. I was very unhappy in

Weston-Super-Mare and wondered if my "visions" were just an extension of my unhappiness.

We moved to this region but were soon troubled by poltergeist activity. We called in a medium, who said that the activity stemmed from me. A lot of unwanted paranormal activity happens around me, but it is my dreams that trouble me most. For example, as a child, I dreamed that my grandmother would die on her thirtieth birthday at 7:30. She lived for another twelve years but died at 7:30 a.m. on *my* thirtieth birthday.

I now have vivid dreams that my husband is going to die. I see the funeral in precise detail. Do you think that this could be another dreadful premonition?

—C. S. N.

I agree with the medium who said that *you* are the source of the paranormal activity. In particular, poltergeist activity can be caused by the release of pent-up psychic energy. Elsewhere in your letter, you say how your marriage has been through some difficulties. The dreams about your husband dying are more likely to be symbolic of the repressed fears you have about state of your relationship than portents for the future. When you have resolved the emotional conflicts in your relationship, the bad dreams will cease.

AN INVISIBLE HAND PROVES MY FRIEND IS SAFE.

One evening, I was sitting at home reading when out of the corner of my eye I saw a movement. When I looked, it was as if an invisible hand had taken a slim booklet from the bookcase and was now carrying it through the air! The floating object fell to the floor and landed at my feet. Somewhat shaken, I picked it up and read it. It was a programme for a theatre play that I had seen ages ago with my friend Ann, who was a medium from Bristol.

An hour later, the phone rang. It was bad news from Bristol. My friend Anne had died suddenly at exactly the same time that I saw the programme float across the room.

—Stanley L.

Some people would be scared to death to see an object float across the room in the way you described. As a medium, Ann would know that death is not the end and that a better life awaits us beyond the grave. The floating programme was her way of letting you know that her spirit continued. She must have been a remarkable medium to be able to use her powers in this way so soon after dying. And I'm sure her communication brought you some comfort.

MY SPOOKY TABLE

Beside my bed, I have a heavy table. Every night for two or three years, it would move about four inches by itself. I began to imagine that someone I cared for was trying to get in touch with me from the other side. Three years ago, the movements stopped, only to be replaced by a knocking noise. Sometimes the table knocks softly, and at other times it is quite loud. It continues throughout the night at intervals of between five and fifteen minutes. Can you explain it?

—Mr. J. B.

Although it could be the contracting of the table's wood that causes the sound, it has been known for spirit people to use tables to communicate with the living. A group of mediums will sit with their hands on a table. It will either tilt to tap out messages with its legs, or make a knocking sound to answer questions. I've tried it myself, and it works, but I would advise that only skilled mediums try this technique, as your own thoughts can influence the messages.

LIGHT BULB LEVITATES

Two years ago, my auntie died, and it broke my heart, as we were very close. At night, as I am just about to fall asleep, I feel someone standing next to me by the bed. I always smell this beautiful perfume. One evening, I opened my eyes, and the light bulb—which was still on—floated from its socket and landed on the floor. It remained alight!
What do you think this means?
—Mary H.

The beautiful perfume is often called a "psychic breeze," a term first used by the medium Doris Stokes. A loved one from the spirit side will make their presence known by their familiar perfume or aftershave. I've never witnessed a disconnected bulb light up by itself, but we have seen very bright spirit lights float in the room.

MEDIUM HELPS OUT

It all started when I began to feel a chill down my left side. Then things started to fall off the shelves by themselves. At first, I just laughed it off, but gradually the problems got worse. The lights started to behave strangely, things started to disappear, the video often started by itself, and I kept hearing a rattling sound and eerie voices. Every time that I thought I saw something out of the corner of my eye, our Rottweiler dog would shake with fear.
I had visited a medium some time before, so I rang her, and she agreed to pay a visit to see what she could do. Just before she arrived, an ornament slid off

the television and scared the life out of me. It took her a while to calm me down.

She said that she felt there was a presence there, and then we all heard this loud, scraping sound go across the ceiling. The medium reassured me that our spirit visitor was, in fact, my grandfather, and she then proceeded to tell me all about him. She said that he was concerned over the problems that I was having in my marriage. I'm still a bit jumpy, but if it really is my grandfather, then there is no problem. What do you think?

—June T.

I expect that the medium is right. Some people will jump with fright at the slightest hint of paranormal events. Now you know that the spirit means no harm, you may take comfort in the things happening around you. Also, when we are emotionally upset we can mysteriously move objects ourselves by the angry energy we project.

DID A GHOST WRECK OUR KITCHEN?

I recently had a frightening experience while staying at my sister's house. At 5:00 a.m. in the morning, we heard a crashing coming from the kitchen. When we went downstairs, the place was a mess. Most of the kitchen items were all over the floor—the ironing board, bottles, cleaning items, the brush. Things were strewn everywhere, yet before we had gone to bed, we had tidied up and put everything securely away.

Strange things have happened in this house ever since my mother gave me an old coffee table. Recently we looked underneath it and found the letters of an Ouija board, chalked in a circle underneath it. Do you think that this table caused

these strange phenomena? We have since thrown it away.

—Isabelle P.

Poltergeist activity has often been linked to Ouija boards. If a restless earth-bound entity saw it as their only means of communication, they may have expressed their frustration through psychokinetic activity. The more likely explanation is that something inadvertently fell from the recently tidied cupboards and caused the mess.

4 SÉANCES AND OUIJA BOARDS

GUIDED TO A SÉANCE

This story, which took place when I was a young lady, may seem unbelievable, but it really happened. We had just finished our Sunday tea when I announced to my mother that I must go out immediately. I put on my hat and coat and walked down the street, not knowing quite where I was heading. It was as if I were in a vacuum or trance-like state.

I went up some steps and knocked on a door. A lady let me in and led me to an almost pitch-dark room, where I was shown to a seat. I had no idea where I was or why I was there, but was told afterwards that it was a séance. A person stood in the middle of the circle, about 5 feet 7 inches high, who seemed to be in control of proceedings. Now this is the marvellous part. From the man arose another man's head and shoulders. It was my "dead" father, with his distinctive moustache, and wearing his fur-lined waistcoat and black-and-white chequered pants. I wasn't afraid at all. He said that I must not worry about him and that he was happy.

Everybody there had someone come to visit them. There were old women, a man with a stick, a soldier, young girls, etc. For some, the short man spoke and gave messages from the apparitions.

Nowadays, if I want to see the spirit people, my own room goes cold, and I look round and there they are.

—Mrs. T.

You really jumped in at the deep end. You had visited a psychic circle in which the spirit communicator materialised—probably out of ectoplasm, a white, misty substance that forms from the demonstrating medium's body. To be guided to a meeting like this, without even knowing what a séance was, is in itself remarkable. There are many mediums like myself who would give their right arm to experience what you did that evening. Have any other readers seen physical mediumship?

I SAW IT WITH MY OWN EYES

You mentioned in your column that you'd like to hear from people who have witnessed physical mediumship first hand. My mother took me to visit a spiritualist group that met in Surrey, and this was my first encounter with anything "paranormal."

I saw things that would amaze you. A trumpet rose into the air by itself, and spirit voices spoke through it. One of those voices I recognised—it was my father's, with an important and meaningful message for me.

I also saw objects moving and witnessed a stream of ectoplasm stream from the medium's head and transform into a hand. This disembodied hand then took off the jacket of the medium, who was securely tied to a chair, and carried it to the other side of the room.

Many readers will think these things impossible, but I saw them with my own eyes. Indeed, many famous people saw similar things, e.g. Donald Pearson, Sir Oliver Lodge, and Willam Crookes. I am encouraged to know that people are becoming more tolerant of this knowledge and are now sincerely looking for the truth.

—Margaret C.

Physical mediumship was a remarkable phenomenon that has all but disappeared. Are there any groups out there who are prepared to write to me about physical materialisation that is happening *today*? Or maybe have you have a ghostly photograph to show us. Write to me at the usual address.

I CONTACTED MY DEAD MOTHER WITH THE OUIJA BOARD

My daughter married and moved to England. Her mother-in-law reads Tarot cards and is exceptionally good. She does not do this for money.

On a visit to my daughter's, I was astonished to learn that on her last visit, three of them had used a glass surrounded by the alphabet, together with a "Yes" and a "No," to contact spirits. I believe that this is called an Ouija board.

After much coaxing and a few drinks, we tried it again and were contacted by her father and mother. Since then I have spoken to my Mum, grandmother, uncle, father-in-law, etc. Afterwards my deceased grandmother, who was a true Christian in every sense, ended with, "God bless you."

My question is: Is it all right to use this board, and is there a danger that an evil spirit may use it?

The Ouija board is a very effective method of spirit communication but is rarely used nowadays. It is an uncontrolled form of spirit communication and requires a powerful, well-trained medium in charge for it to work without encountering problems. Should an earth-bound or malevolent spirit slip through, you may find it hard to get rid of. This can be very frightening if you are not properly trained.

HORROR IN THE MIRROR

I am worried for myself and my friends, as an experiment we did with the Ouija board has gone badly wrong. At first we were in contact with a nice old lady called Nessie, but after a few sessions, she gradually started to spell out a load of nonsense. Later, a man calling himself Paul started to communicate. He said that he was a murderer and had been hanged for his crimes. His messages were full of hate and, to our horror, his distorted face appeared in the mirror, and the candles flared up.

All of us are terrified, as we now see and feel him following us to our homes. This letter is not a joke. We are really very worried.
—Alan D.

The Ouija board can be extremely dangerous in untrained hands, and you must urge your friends to stop at once. Meanwhile, protect yourselves by visualising a bright, loving light around your aura, as darkness cannot penetrate light. I will be getting in touch with you directly to see if I can sort the problem out.

THE ENIGMA OF PHYSICAL MEDIUMSHIP

There have been several times when a misty form has floated above me as I was lying in bed. This has

happened for over twenty years now and always fills me with fear.

One night I was woken by my wife, who was gripping my arm tightly. We were terrified to see, standing at the bottom of our bed, two figures. Both were hooded. At my wife's feet stood a white figure, and at my feet stood a black figure. This was not the first time we had seen these strange forms. Prior to this we could both see dark, hooded figures walk in a circle in the darkness; sometimes one of the figures would lean over our daughter's cot, and she would wake up screaming.

We have tried joining a circle to communicate with this spirit, and even used a Ouija board to get in touch, but our questions about these forms just haven't been solved. When we used the board, a beautiful perfume filled the room, and small, white dust flakes filled the tumbler. My wife would receive electric shocks when she touched it, and she would be exhausted after a session. Can you explain these occurrences?

—William B.

Many of the things you have described have the hallmark of what the Spiritualists call "physical mediumship." Sir Arthur Conan Doyle, the author of the Sherlock Holmes stories, devoted a great deal of his life to the study of this phenomenon.

Physical mediumship starts with a mist—called ectoplasm—that emanates from the medium. As the power grows, this mist can build to form a complete, solid figure of someone from the spirit world. The ectoplasm forms in sheet-like ripples, and many of the photographs that were taken during the 1930s reveal the figures to appear hooded.

There have been many reports over the last few years of this remarkable form of mediumship starting to happen again. Even though you have been frightened by the phenomenon, you have had twenty years to learn that at no time these figures have ever harmed you. They won't— so don't be frightened.

WILL I DIE AT SIXTY-FIVE?

Many years ago, when I was a teenager, some friends and I started playing about with the Ouija board. When we "made contact," we took turns to ask the spirit some questions, and when it came to my turn, I stupidly asked the spirit when and how I would die. It answered through the board that I would die at sixty-five, and it would be in a plane crash.

Now much older and wiser, I realise that dabbling in these things can be dangerous. However, I would like to know if the spirit could have been right, or if (as I have read in a book) spirits don't have access to this information.

You will appreciate that this is causing me some anxiety.

—Joseph S.

The time and manner of our death is not accessible through any form of clairvoyance. Many of the phenomena displayed through Ouija boards come from a collective telepathy, and the messages can reflect our own inner fears.

PUBLIC RECORDS DEPARTMENT CONFIRMS SPIRIT RETURN

I have been using the glass and letter circle and have been told that I have an Indian guide called Qooqtor. I have been told some remarkable things that have come true and that I should look to join a circle.

Through the glass, I was told that a family member would become pregnant, but the person they would marry would not be the father. Three months later, this came to pass. My grandmother also communicated and spoke of a twin son, named Robert, whom she had lost a few weeks after his birth. No one living knew his name, so I checked at the department of records. To my surprise, there it was in black and white: "Robert"!

—Sheila F.

The Society of Psychical Research would find your case interesting. Many of the objections to spirit communication are that the medium may be telepathically reading the minds of the sitters. As no one living knew of Robert, it goes a long way toward demonstrating that you *did* contact people in the afterlife.

CONTACTING THE HIGHER PLANES

Your readers' letters, and books I have read, would suggest that we humans live at the bottom of a series of well-defined planes. Our gross material plane is directly below the psychic plane, where astral travel can occur and spirits reside. How can we contact the higher planes?

—Duncan D.

Some call these planes the "cosmic spheres." The Buddhists call them the *bardos*, and the poet W. B. Yeats, who belonged to the mystical group called the Golden Dawn, called them the gyres. As a soul develops spiritually, it progresses into the higher planes, but can also come back to guide and help others. Advanced souls are claimed to be the spirit controls of many trance mediums. David Icke was convinced that he spoke to Socrates and Plato through the mediumship of Betty Shine—but there again, he claimed a lot of strange things.

THE PROBLEM'S GETTING WORSE

I am another of the people involved with the "Ouija danger" letter, as printed in the paper. We have stopped using the board, as you advised, but the problems continue. Things keep moving by themselves. The light bulb blew, and a set of keys flew four feet across the room and hit me. The keys didn't hurt half as much as the shock of it happening! The last straw is that a menacing figure now appears in my dreams. He grabs me by the leg, and I awake to find red finger-marks across my leg. The last time this happened, an old lady appeared and drove him away. I described her and how she was dressed to my father, who knows of our problem, and he explained that this was his mother, whom I never knew.

—P. H.

Your grandmother is helping you from the other side. Just as there can be malevolent spirits, we can also call upon very powerful good spirits to help us. Call upon, and have faith in, the invincible power of good. Your grandmother will bring other protective forces to your aid if you send her your thoughts. Meet again with your friends, and instead of using the board, visualise a golden light of protection between you. The advanced spirit beings—which some call angels—will come to your aid.

RIGHT HAND KNOWS WHAT LEFT IS DOING

I have a suggestion that may help the lady with the Ouija board problem.

Firstly, they must find out who brought the negative thought to the Ouija board, so that "Paul" will not feed from their fear and get stronger.

The strongest sister should act as the speaker. Hold hands and take a deep breath, visualising it as a cleansing breath of loving light. As you exhale, expel all the disharmony from your bodies. Repeat five to seven times.

Each person should then send loving thoughts through their left hand to the person next to them, until the power of love builds. Now visualise yourselves surrounded in a beautiful light, until you are comfortable. Then ask the board for the protection of a guiding spirit to help appease the spirit of "Paul."

—Robert

Our readers have no doubt become aware of the dangers that can be caused by Ouija boards. In the right hands it can be a useful tool, but if you don't know what you're doing, then *don't* use it!

5 MESSAGES FROM THE DEAD

PASSING OVER THE MACE

Reading some of the letters in your column, I am reminded of an experience that happened to me ten years ago and has puzzled with me ever since.

At the time, I was employed by a local borough council, and one of my duties was to act as deputy to the Mace-bearer (Sergeant-at-Mace) which, among other things, involves escorting the Lord Mayor to civic functions.

I remember my friend, the Mace-bearer, taking me aside and saying, "One day, there'll be a nice pair of shoes for you to step into." Presumably he meant that I'd be his successor.

Eight months later, I dreamed that my telephone was ringing. I answered it and across a hissing line heard a faint and distant voice. "It's all yours now, Mike." I knew it was my friend, the Mace-bearer, and I tried to question him but only heard a sound akin to "white noise."

I was awoken in the morning by my front door bell. It was another colleague who had been sent from

the council offices. He had come to inform me that the Mace-bearer had passed away the night before!
—Michael C. (Sergeant-at-Mace)

Your friend and predecessor obviously loved his job and wanted you to inherit his position. One of his last earthly duties was to inform you of the job vacancy. I believe that many traditions are continued in the spirit world. For example, I have myself often given mediumistic messages from spirit people who, as proof of their identity, have shown themselves dressed in full Masonic regalia. I presume that if Freemasonry continues in the afterlife, then so does the tradition of the Mace-bearing.

EVERY PICTURE TELLS A STORY

I was devastated when my father died of a heart attack in 1988. It was as if my life went on hold, and it took me a long time to resolve my grief. But something happened that lifted my spirits and gave me the strength to go on.

I was sitting with my boyfriend, watching television, when I glanced up at the painting of a hunt scene that Dad had bought me some time ago. It's almost impossible to describe what happened next, but the painting came alive, and I was transported inside it.

Ahead of me I could see a path that led to a garden shed. Sitting outside of this was my father. He was dressed in his best suit, his shoes shone like fire, and his hair was immaculate. He looked in perfect health.

As I ran towards him, I was aware that we were surrounded by a beautiful garden. "Don't worry about me," I heard him whisper as I drew close.

I was about to step over a little garden trellis to where he stood, but he stopped me. As he did this, I "awoke" and was back sitting on the sofa in front of

the picture. For me, this "vision" was the turning point, and I could now start living my life again.
—Miss Angela P.

Your father communicated to you through a waking dream. I find these stories of pictures that come alive intriguing. One of the most remarkable was sent to me by two identical twin sisters from Scotland. Their "dead" mother communicated to them in the same way as your father did, except they were drawn into the picture together and described an identical vision.

MUM BREAKS THE NEWS

When my husband was in the army, he had an affair. He admitted this to me and said that there was a pregnancy, which we were told came to nothing. Thirty years later, I started "seeing" my mother's ghost. She seemed to be trying to tell me something.

I became so concerned that I even went to her grave and asked: "What's the matter, Mum? What are you trying to tell me?"

Shortly after these spirit visits, we received a shocking phone call. My husband had a daughter who was now thirty years old! I know that Mum will come again if I need her. Without her warning, the shock would have been far worse.
—Mrs Edith T.

Clearly your mother's spirit was trying to prepare you for the unexpected news. Your marriage survived your husband's unfaithfulness from so long ago. You are a loyal and tolerant lady. May your daughter-in-law bring you unexpected happiness.

NERVOUS SPIRIT PROJECTION SAYS "CHEERIO"

What happened to me on a Sunday, eighteen months ago, has so impressed me that the experience feels as if it only just happened yesterday. The television was on but, as it was a repeat, I decided to read. Then I heard the distinctive voice of my brother-in-law. "It's all right," I heard him say.

I looked up. About six feet away was what I can only describe as a projection of him. He wore a green checked shirt and brown trousers. He looked a little nervous and was wringing his hands. He spoke again: "I've come round to say 'Cheerio.' Now it's my turn to go." And then he just disappeared into thin air.

Although I had heard that he had gone into hospital, I had no idea that he was so seriously ill. I had my "vision" of him at 7:43 p.m. My brother-in-law had died only moments ago at 7:30. In addition, my son, whom I hadn't spoken to, saw the spirit at his house at 2:00 p.m. Again, my brother-in-law was wringing his hands.

At the time I was relaxed and, of course, sober. My astonishing experience was as real as day. I would be prepared to take a lie detector test to prove that what I saw was absolutely real.

—Mr. Charles A.

I'm sure that you're telling the truth. Most of the reports of spirit sightings come at the time of, or near to, a death. You can hardly believe how real it is when the spirit world is able to manifest directly to you. You must find it very reassuring to have such convincing proof that your brother-in-law's spirit has survived bodily death.

MY DEAD SISTER SAVED MY DAUGHTER'S LIFE

My daughter looked quite shaken when she arrived at my house. She explained that, as she drove, she saw in her mirror someone sitting on the back seat of the car. She stepped on the brake and turned around to see the spirit of her auntie smiling at her. It then vanished as quickly as it appeared. When she drove on, she came upon a dreadful road accident. If she'd been seconds earlier, then the accident would have happened to her own vehicle.

To this day my daughter believes that her dead auntie saved her life.

—Gladys W.

It is the power of love that fuels the spiritual communication between the worlds. I am aware that your sister loved her niece very much. I'm sure that she's right. Her life was saved by the dead.

MY DEAD FATHER PREDICTED MY MOTHER'S ILLNESS

Soon after my father died, I had an early morning dream about him. He joked, as he did in life, had a silver light around him, and when he reached out and touched my hands, he felt warm and normal. "It's true! There is an afterlife!" I exclaimed in my dream. "Have you met Auntie Alice and Grandma Coates?" I asked.

"Of course I have" replied my father. "But there's something very important that I must tell you. Mum is not well; she must attend to her chest."

I had to wait until Mum returned from holiday before I could tell her about the dream. "I'm fine," she said. "There's nothing wrong with me." But I persisted when I noticed a nasty red lump on her chest. I insisted that she visit the doctor to get it checked.

The lump was cancerous. Mum had radiation treatment at St. Mary's Hospital, and the cancer was caught just in time. She is now ninety years old and as fit as a fiddle.

—Jennifer T.

Dreams that happen in the early-morning dream phase are often the most vivid. At these times, some people have "lucid dreams," which are as clear as waking awareness.

It could be argued that your subconscious mind may have already observed your mother's red lump and told you about it in a dream. But I believe the simpler answer: Your father's spirit communicated to save your mother's life. Communication with the afterlife can sometimes be very useful.

DO GHOSTS HAVE ANSWERING MACHINES?

The man I loved died suddenly from a stroke. He was separated from his wife while we were together, but I felt that it would be best not to go to the funeral, as it might upset some of the family.

For days before the funeral, I was torn between whether to go or not, and felt terribly upset. There I was, wondering what to do, when I heard this lovely soft voice say: "Sorry we are not in at the moment due to the funeral, but if you would like to join the entourage at the crematorium, you will be most welcome. Thanks for calling."

I could not believe what was happening, but it was definitely his voice I heard, with its soft accent. He used to joke a lot and used to get cross with me if I didn't leave a message on his answering machine. It was a standing joke between us. Do you think that

this was his way of making a very personal message to me, or is it just my imagination?
—Edith B.

Mediums are often accused of relaying messages that are both trivial and meaningless. Critics would, no doubt, class a message about an answering machine in this category. However, for you it was a very poignant and evidential message that only your loved one and yourself would know.

You do not tell us whether the voice that you heard was inside your head or disembodied. Nonetheless, it would be fair to assume that your humorous partner would like to reassure you that it was alright to attend the funeral in a way most fitting to his character.

TEA FOR TWO

I keep having vivid dreams of the dead. The most unusual one concerned my deceased father-in-law. He was laughing and said that he'd come for a free cup of tea, and handed me a distinctive red-and-black tin. I awoke with streams of happy tears running down my face.

Later I told my mother about the dream. She rummaged at the back of the cupboard beneath the sink and produced a red-and-black tin that was identical in patterning to the one shown me in my dream.
—Dawn B.

Obviously your father-in-law had a good sense of humour. He reached you through your subconscious mind in your dream and gave you and your mother excellent proof of his survival.

WE BOTH HEARD MY MOTHER'S CALL

A week after my mother died, my sister and I were clearing out our mother's things. I went to cut out the obituary from the paper, thinking that my son would like to keep it. Then we both heard Mother's voice call out my name! We were totally shocked. Do you think Mother was trying to tell us not to send the clipping?
—Mrs. M. MacD.

Your mother just wanted to let you all know that she was alright. The obituary clipping is a proof of her death, but for you both to hear her spirit voice is a proof of her new life. Tell your son about what you heard.

SOUVENIR RETURNS

My sister always likes to buy a little souvenir when she goes on holiday or visits somewhere special. When she went on holiday with her Aunt Ethel, she bought an edelweiss broach, but on her return home somehow lost it. Years later there was a crash in the kitchen, and my sister went to find out what had fallen. In the middle of the floor was the edelweiss broach that she lost so many years ago. As she picked it up and remembered her holiday with Ethel, the telephone rang. Her daughter answered it. "Mum," she called out. "That call was to let you know that Auntie Ethel died half an hour ago."
—Mr. Len B.

Sometimes when a group of mediums sit in a séance together, the psychic power can become so intense that objects will materialise from nowhere. The sitters at the séances of the famous medium Mrs. Guppy used to witness objects appear nearly every time they met. On one winter's evening, a sunflower plant—roots and all—fell from the ceiling. Whether paranormal powers materialised the broach or not is not as important as the remarkable timing of the event.

I'M NO LONGER A SCEPTIC

I was always very sceptical about psychic powers, and especially mediums. On June 8 this year, I visited the Spiritualist Church for the very first time. The visiting medium gave me a perfect description of my dearest friend, who had died, together with his age and the exact date of his death. All I can say to those who don't want to believe in the spirit world is, go to a medium with an open mind and listen. I came out a changed man.
—Patrick J. L.

I'm glad that you met a first-class medium and got a clear message straightaway.

PLEASE FORGIVE ME

Soon after my husband died, I found proof that he had been having an affair. It left me emotionally tormented. I went into town for the day to take my mind off things, but just wandered aimlessly, and by the time I got home, I was very upset and my spirits were very low indeed. When I went into the bedroom, there I saw my husband's photograph, lying face down in the middle of the room. The frame was very sturdy, and there was no way it could have fallen the way it did.
—Edith W.

You have conflicting feeling of grief and anger towards your departed husband that must be emotionally draining.

If he moved the photo, then he must be trying to seek your forgiveness.

FALSE TEETH PROVE LIFE AFTER DEATH

Sometimes it seems as if my spirit leaves my body, and when this happens, I see people I have known who have passed away. On one occasion I saw my mother. She was pointing at her top teeth. I checked with Dad, and he said that Mother had died with only the top set of her false teeth in. I feel that I can't get on with my own life until I have coped with their deaths.

—Carol D.

Mother proved that it was really her by telling you something that you could check. Now you know that she is okay, she would want you to get on with life and let go of the past.

TUNED INTO THE BLITZ

During World War Two, my work as a medium was in great demand. As well as helping the bereaved, I used to sit every night and attune myself in order to help the dying servicemen enter the afterlife. I had spirit communications from troops and the French resistance, and in particular I recall the many spirit communications that happened on the night Coventry was blitzed.

One of the most interesting pieces of proof we had concerned my husband's dream. He saw himself on board an aeroplane with his young friend. In the dream he realised that the plane had been hit by enemy fire and that the crew were about to die. Some days later, we received news that the plane had been hit at the time of the dream and that my husband's friend had died.

—Mrs. Jenny G.

Dreams are a rich source of psychic experience and are a time when our Extra Sensory Perceptions (ESP) are awake. The world wars were times when many people like yourself engaged in regular communication with the afterlife. Even Air Marshal Lord Dowding was a keen Spiritualist.

DEAD FRIEND REVEALS LOTTERY WIN

When my very dear friend died, I was able to tell the doctors the exact moment of his death. And after he'd gone it was as if his spirit had never left me. Throughout life we had shared the same likes and dislikes, and even spoke the same thoughts at the same moment. We were as close as twin brothers.

My friend had left me his possessions, and it was my job to sort through everything and dispose of any rubbish. I wanted to get the trauma over with as soon as possible, so I gathered all the letters and papers together into a pile ready to throw out.

But a clear voice interrupted my work. "Alf, you know I don't want it done that way. Sort through everything before you throw things away."

The voice was so insistent that I dared not disobey. And it's just as well I listened to the phantom voice. Among the paperwork were the records of a fairly substantial lottery win that my friend had kept secret.

But better than the money is the certain knowledge that my beloved friend is close.

—Alf W.

One of the things sceptics say to psychics is, "Okay, if you're so psychic, how come you don't predict the lottery numbers for yourself?'

Next time they sneer, I think I'll quote your little story of how your dead friend help you hit the jackpot.

PSYCHIC DISCOVERY NETS HARD CASH

A few days after Dad died, I went to his house to begin sorting out some of his things. Perhaps it was Dad's spirit influencing me, but for some inexplicable reason I felt drawn to the heavy wardrobe in the bedroom. I just had to look underneath it.

How I found the strength to move it, I just do not know. Underneath one of the legs, I could feel a loose floorboard beneath the lino. I lifted the corner of the plank and pulled out a small package. Inside was £2,000 in £20 pound notes!

I had absolutely no prior knowledge that would have made me want to move the wardrobe, so I'm sure that it was Dad who led me to my inheritance.

—Mrs Joyce S.

It's lucky that you were psychic enough to "hear" the message from your father, or a considerable amount of money would have gone to waste. I'm sure that it was Dad's spirit that helped you make the discovery.

THE GRAVEYARD SHIFT

I recently visited my father's grave in the late afternoon. It was getting late as I left, and the cemetery supervisor unlocked the gates for me. "Where's the old gentleman in the white raincoat?" he asked

Puzzled, I asked him what he meant. "The one with a limp, who walked beside you as you just came

down this path." Nobody else appeared, and he locked the gates behind me, unaware that he had perfectly described my late father!
—**Mervyn S.**

The clairvoyant cemetery supervisor unknowingly gave you the reassurance of knowing that Dad is with you when you visit his grave.

6 STRANGE SPIRITS

EVERY PICTURE TELLS A STORY

Last September, I was hanging wallpaper and feeling very depressed, as things had not been going well for me at that time. A portrait photo fell from the wall. I picked it up and spoke the person's name as I did so. To my astonishment, someone I knew with the same name as the person in the photograph was standing right in front of me. But he had been dead for years!

He wore the same clothes as when I knew him, except they appeared brighter, and he had the same hair-style. His face, though, looked strange, as if it had a thin film over it. He stayed for a few more seconds then disappeared. Despite the strangeness of the event, I wasn't frightened at all.

Why did this happen? Do you think that he was trying to tell me something?
—Peter S.

Although you have not told us exactly who the spirit person was, he must have cared for you a great deal. Clearly you were depressed at the time, and by calling his name you triggered a communication with his spirit. I expect that he wanted to bring you comfort in your time of distress. Even though his face was indistinct, he was able to communicate enough detail to let you know that he was with you.

IS MY DEAD MOTHER TRYING TO GET IN TOUCH?

I washed the curtains in my conservatory, hung them back up, and next day found that they had fallen to the floor. Also, I washed my net curtains from another room and found that the wire had come off the hooks, and these too had fallen down.

Both these events happened on the third anniversary of my mother's death. Do you think that there is a connection?

—Heather D.

I'm afraid my verdict is that the weight of the water left in the curtains probably caused them to break free. We can't explain every unusual occurrence as paranormal. But that doesn't necessarily mean that your mother didn't draw close to you on this special anniversary. I'm sure her love is very much around you.

A WASTED YOUNG LIFE

My niece recently died at the young age of only twenty-five. A question mark still hangs over her death, as it is suspected that she took her own life.

A few days after the funeral, her little sister had a vision. She saw a bright light, with a stairway ascending into the air. On it, she saw her sister running and dancing. The figure turned to face her, gave a bright happy smile, and then disappeared. She was, she says, overwhelmed with a feeling of

happiness and well-being. Do you think that this was a real vision of my niece's spirit, or was it just a result of the stress caused by the tragic events?

—B. S.

I can't say for certain whether the insight was a direct communication with the afterlife or a wishful fulfilment vision. However, I can assure you that, in my experience, spirit communicators who have taken their own life are not punished in the next world. They regret their mistake but usually try to reassure the living that, despite their foolishness, they are happy.

A MESSAGE FROM HEAVEN

On the night my mother died, my son, aged thirty-two, had a vision. As he awoke from a dream, the bedroom door swung open, and there stood my Mum, arm-in-arm with Dad. My son had never met his grandfather, who died before he was born, yet he was able to give an accurate description of him.

A few weeks later, as my son was driving along the Guildford bypass, he sensed that my dead mother-in-law was with him in the car. He described smelling her perfume mixed with Dettol (she always washed with a little Dettol in the water). Was she trying to give my son a message?

A few months later, my husband was taken seriously ill and died. I coped with the grief, but on Easter morning fell into a deep depression. "If only I knew that my husband was alright," I prayed.

When my son got up, he eagerly told me about another dream he had just had. "I was on a motorway bridge," he said. "Dad was standing there and, even though I knew he was dead, I ran towards him. "I do miss you and Mum so much," said Dad. "Tell her that the afterlife is just like the earth except far, far more beautiful. We have seasons with sun and rain, just like on earth. And I now live in a picturesque little village, like you find in Scotland. Tell Mum that I'm happy and that one day we'll all be together again."

I feel that my son's dream was an answer to my prayer.

—Mrs R.

Your son appears to be very psychic and should consider developing his gift. He's already brought comfort to you. He could also bring comfort to others. Many readers may find it difficult to accept that the afterlife is a glorious version of this world. But it's not just wishful thinking—the afterlife, say we psychics, is a parallel dimension, one of many levels of existence that lie beyond the material world.

GHOSTLY POSTMAN

Some weeks ago my niece, who was visiting Germany, wrote to me to ask where she could find the grave of my nephew, who died after being interned there in WW2. I searched for the documents but could not find them.

One night, I couldn't sleep and, to my amazement, I saw an elderly Scot standing in front of the antique writing desk that I had recently inherited. He wore a red plaid kilt and a small black vest and jacket, and his long, silver-grey hair was brushed back in waves. In his hand he held a letter. As I stared at him, he slowly faded away.

Next day I searched the desk thoroughly and found a picture of this mysterious Scot, exactly as I had seen him in my vision. Attached to the photo was an old letter from the War Commission with all the information that my niece required.

—Rose C.

Your interesting story, which involves spirit communication across more than one country, reminds us of the famous experiment called the "cross correspondence." Frederick Myers, a founder member of the Society for Psychical Research, left with his colleague, Sir Oliver Lodge, an envelope containing a code that was not to be opened until well after his death. When he died, he would relay the message through a medium. Remarkably, the Latin message was relayed bit by bit from all over the world and as far away as India. Mediums that knew nothing of the experiment that was taking place gave Myers' name and messages through automatic writing, Ouija boards, and trance.

MY HUSBAND CAME TO ME

Soon after my husband died, I would hear voices in my bedroom. I would keep my eyes tightly closed, too scared to have a look. Then I heard a very clear voice say, "Let Mrs. J. sleep." When I finally opened my eyes, I clearly saw my husband standing beside my bed. I reached out to touch him, and he vanished with a swishing noise. I saw my husband so very, very clearly—what I have written is absolutely true. There were many troubles between us before he passed, and I didn't deserve his harsh treatment, so why is he trying so hard to communicate with me?
—Mrs Dorothy J.

I have abridged your letter to preserve your confidentiality but feel strongly that your husband wants to make his peace with you. It wasn't until he reached the other side of life, and saw things in a wider perspective, that he realised how much he loved you.

DAD'S GUIDANCE

When my husband was told that he was to lose his job and that we should make plans to leave the cottage that went with it, you can imagine how worried we were. We were to be made redundant and homeless at the same time.

A few days after the bad news, I saw the spirit of my father appear in the cottage. He looked happy, as if he wanted to give me some good news. He was a lovely man. Soon after we received a phone call: the council had allotted us another cottage. It's a lovely place, and we live in it to this day.

—Ellen G.

At times of adversity, the spirit world can sometimes come to reassure us that we need not worry. Your father wanted to let you know that as one door closes, another opens.

PSYCHIC MESSAGE

I dreamed of my friend who had passed. He wore a white suit. Do you think that he was trying to get in touch with me?

—Marion B.

People in the spirit world don't wear white, sit around on clouds, and play the harp. However, they may appear to us dressed in white as a symbol of the peace that they have found. When we are asleep, it is easier for the spirit friends to communicate with us, and we feel that your friend did try to reach you.

AFTER-LIFE, AFTER-SHAVE

I feel that my father's spirit has been around me, as sometimes I smell the familiar scent of his after-shave. He lost his leg just before he died, and I dreamed one night that he returned to me to say that he'd got his leg back. Some years later, my mother was taken terminally ill, and before passing she exclaimed that Dad was in the room, and that he now had both legs. Do you think that what we both saw was true?

—Mary G.

Many Christians believe that the dead sleep in the grave, awaiting the day of judgement. However, the evangelist preacher Dr. Billy Graham has described a similar event to yours His dying grandmother sat up in bed and saw her dead husband, Ben, who had lost a leg and an eye in the Civil War. She said, "There is Ben, and he has both his eyes and both his legs!"

BROTHER RETURNS FROM THE DEAD

Late one night, there was a knock at my door. I looked through the peephole and asked who was there. A man said that he was looking for his sister, Evelyn, and gave his name as Karl C. I opened the door and was shocked to see my brother. He had died some years ago on the eve of his ninetieth birthday! He told me things about his life and asked me why I hadn't visited him at the Royal Infirmary when he was dying. As I looked at him, he became younger—just as I remembered him when he was twenty.

—Evelyn N.

When a spirit person makes a return, it is not always as a wispy transparent form. Some people see them as solid. Your experience sounds remarkably real.

THROUGH THE LOOKING GLASS

One night, while I was staying at my grandmother's house, I was looking in the mirror and saw my dead grandfather standing behind me. I went to turn round, and he disappeared. Can you explain what happened that night?
—Mrs. Gloria M.

Reports have recently been coming from America about the latest psychic experiments by Dr. Raymond Moody. He is famous for his clinical studies of Near-Death Experiences. Now he has started experimenting with spirit contact. His subjects sit in a dark room in front of a mirror, tilted at an angle to the ceiling. Faces of the dead appear. Your Grandad used this same technique.

LIFEBOATS TO THE RESCUE

One evening, my sister and I were walking along the high wall at the harbour, when we saw the image of our father float out of the water. (He had died in 1943, trying to rescue someone in a lifeboat). He jumped out of the sea and spoke to both of us. "I have come to look after you. Fancy a whisky at the Plough and Harrow?" We both heard his words and saw him. Then he jumped back into the sea and disappeared. We return to the same place every night in the hope that he will appear to us again.
—E. S. and N. L.

Clearly, your father was a brave man with a sense of humour. In death, as in life, he still comes to the rescue when he hears the call.

MY HAIR STOOD ON END

Late one evening, I sat exhausted on the couch, having just fed our new-born baby. I tried to get up but was unable to move. Every hair on my body stood on end, as if I was receiving a bolt of electricity. I could feel someone standing behind me! I tried to call out but couldn't. Then there was a deafening sound, like paper crumpling. With a massive effort, I finally called out, and my husband came downstairs to see what was up.

The experience so frightened me that in the morning I telephoned my Dad. "Did you realise that yesterday was the anniversary of Grandma's death?" he said. She had communicated before, he told me, through séances conducted by my aunt.

—Kate L.

Physical exhaustion triggered your experience—but it was real nonetheless. Grandma is used to communication with the living, so she could make her presence felt very dramatically. It's nothing to be alarmed about.

7 CROSSING OVER

COLD SHIVERS

Throughout my married life, my husband and I have experienced strange psychic phenomena. When we were courting, smoke from a train formed a perfect letter "E" at the moment my aunt—with the same initial—died. We also used to hear the rustle of my dead grandmother's taffeta skirt in the corridor, and my mother would joke that she too would come back and tell us what it was like after she died.

The night my mother died, I was sitting beside her bed in the downstairs front room. Suddenly the room went icy cold. I looked at the fire, but it was bright as ever. Then I saw two ghostly figures walk into the room. I tried to call out to my father and family in the other room, but I was frozen with fright. The figures paused. I noticed that they had no reflection. "Don't be frightened," a quiet voice said to me. "We are Mum's mother and sister. We have come for her. Don't be afraid."

The figures vanished, the room became warm again, and I shouted for my father. Dad rushed into the room and took Mother's hand as she peacefully died.

A few days after the funeral, I awoke with a start. There was a light at the bottom of my bed, which my husband saw as well. Perhaps it was Mum keeping her promise to return and let us know she was alright.

—Margaret G.

I wish there was enough space to print all the stories that you spoke of in your letter, but we'd take over the whole *Weekly News*! You are clearly a very psychic lady indeed and have the makings of a first-class medium—if only someone can train you. On the day of your mother's passing, you saw her loved ones coming for her. On reflection, it must have been very reassuring for you.

LONG LIVE THE KING

At 4:00 a.m. on August 15, 1977, I awoke from a dream that featured Elvis Presley. I was overwhelmed by a feeling of depression and despair, and resolved that I would never play Elvis's records again. Perhaps they were making me depressed. Or was my dream trying to tell me something else: I would never play any *new* Elvis records again, for on the next day (August 16, 1977) Elvis Presley died?

—Pat H.

Did you sense the imminent death of Elvis Presley? His former wife, Priscilla, claims to have seen the King return from beyond the grave. She heard noises coming from the stable and went out to check, where she saw Elvis's favourite horse upset by a "shimmering form, hovering" nearby. And Elvis Presley is said to have foreseen his own tragic death reflected in the pictorial shapes formed in cumulus clouds floating by.

STOP CLOCK

As I was watching television, I glanced at the battery-operated wall clock and noticed that it had stopped at 8:45 p.m. I made a mental note to buy a new battery.

Later that evening, I went into the front room and noticed that the battery-operated clock on the top of the TV had also stopped at exactly 8:45 p.m. I thought this strange. The following day I received a phone call saying that a good friend of mine had unexpectedly died the previous evening. The time of his death was exactly 8:45 p.m.

Coincidence? Or was she telling me of her passing?

—Linda P.

I can hear the sceptics say, "You bought the batteries at the same time, so it's likely that the clocks would stop together." But they haven't read the dozens of our readers' letters that describe exactly the same thing happening to them. I can't believe that this is just coincidence.

OUR HAUNTED HOLIDAY

Our hotel suite at Bembridge on the Isle of Wight was rather big, with two extra beds in the room. During the night, I saw a ghostly figure walk through the door, stop by my bed, and then disappear through the wall. I was half asleep and felt no fear, yet my experience was so real that I shall never forget it. The "ghost" seemed to have a sense of humour and joked about the extra beds in the room.

My husband and I laughed about the experience the next morning as we ate our breakfast. Then the head waiter interrupted us, saying that there was an important call for me at reception from my daughter.

She had some bad news. Last night, my husband's sister had died.

—Mrs D. W., Birmingham

It must be Murphy's Law that weddings, birthdays, Christmas, and holidays are the times to receive bad news. However, your sister-in-law tried not to spoil your fun. She let you know that she was happy, even before you heard that she was "dead."

DAD'S SPIRIT SAYS IT WITH FLOWERS

My eighty-two-year-old father was very ill when my mother and I were summoned to the hospital. Sadly, we arrived fifteen minutes after Dad had passed. We sat with him for half an hour and were very conscious of the strong aroma of flowers in his room.

At my mother's house that evening, after the last visitor had left, the lounge filled with the same potent smell of flowers.

As I was staying at the house that night, I went upstairs to make up a bed. When I returned to the lounge, my mother told me that the whole room had filled with a mist, which was so thick that she could not see the wall on the opposite side of the room. As the mist gradually faded, the aroma disappeared, too.

A few days later, we discovered that the scent had been of wallflowers, my father's favourite flowers.

—Rosemary J. A.

We mediums call this manifestation of scent a "psychic breeze." Many people report smelling a familiar scent helps prove to them that their loved one is close. The thick fog is also commonly reported, but rarely as dense as your mother describes. I have seen this myself when I was investigating a haunted house with a sceptical psychiatrist. When she saw the fog materialise, she nearly died of fright!

MY BROTHER'S FINAL CURTAIN

I woke up in the middle of the night but was unable to move. I couldn't move a muscle and felt very cold. I looked towards the window, and slowly the curtains began to draw by themselves, until they were completely shut. Still unable to move, I then saw them slowly open again.

The next day I received some bad news. My brother had died unexpectedly in his sleep.

—Rosanna B.

Was it the wind that caused the curtains to move by themselves? The event suggests more than coincidence, happening as it did on the night of your brother's death. I believe that your brother was trying to let you know that he had survived death.

TAP DANCING SPIRIT

When my mother was dying, my brother and I took turns watching over her. It was late at night as I sat beside her, and my brother slept on the mat. My mother began to make loud noises, and her mouth started to open more and more. The noises started getting louder and louder.

To help quieten her down and let my exhausted brother sleep, I decided to gently close my mother's mouth by tying a white scarf under her chin and round her head. It did the trick, and she slept soundly. The room was silent.

As I sat beside her, holding her hand, the silence was shattered as the windows flew open. I heard the patter of feet run across the floor and under the bed. The sound of footsteps became that of steel-capped dancing shoes, rhythmically marching around the room.

The noise and clatter awoke my brother, who was also startled to see my mother asleep with the white scarf tied in a bow around her head. The French windows burst open, and the heavy curtains blew in the wind.

My mother died the next night. What do you think was going on that evening?

—D. D., Minehead, Somerset

It must have been quite a shock for your brother to awake as he did. Although the events you describe sound pretty frightening, I think they could all be explained by the wind bursting through the window. Perhaps something light and metallic, like a curtain ring, bounced around the floor. But there again, if I'd been there, I may have thought quite differently.

A BEAUTIFUL GHOST

When my Grandma was ill at home, I stayed at my mother's to help her nurse her. At three o'clock in the morning, I awoke to see an old lady standing by my bed. She was as real as you or me. Her face was beautiful, and she wore black ankle boots, with four buttons at the side; a long, black lace dress trimmed with distinctive, tiny black beads; and a cameo broach. She had long hair, pinned at the back of the neck.

When I reached out to touch her, she disappeared. Surprisingly, I wasn't frightened at all. I lay thinking about what had happened for three hours then finally fell back to sleep.

In the morning, my tear-stained mother explained that during the night my Grandma had died. I told her of my experience of the ghost. She was amazed by my description. It was my Great-Grandma, whom I had never met or seen a photo of. My mother showed me the cameo she wore and the little black beads from her dress, which she had made into a necklace as a memento.

—Sarah M.

We always expect that spirit sightings are of transparent, ghostly forms. But most reports describe the spirit seen as solid and real. Unfortunately I have rarely seen this myself. When spirits communicate through my mediumship, I hear a voice or sense their presence. Your "vision" was so detailed that your mother was clearly able to recognise the spirit. Your Great-Grandma had come for her daughter and had let you know.

MY MOTHER-IN-LAW WENT RIGHT THROUGH ME!

The family gathered around the hospital bed when my mother was dying in hospital. At the foot of the bed stood my brother-in-law. When mother died, he was flung against the wall and exclaimed that something had gone right through him. I was sitting beside Mother, holding her hand, but nothing like that happened to me. Afterwards my brother-in-law looked as white as a sheet.

—Lynn C.

When a person passes, the spirit leaves gently though the top of the head. Unlike you, your brother-in-law may have been very frightened by his first experience of death. He over-reacted.

EARLY MORNING CALL

The morning after my mother died, I got up in the early hours at 5:00 a.m. and sat in the living room. I started to cry. I heard a voice call my name, "Andrew, Andrew." Thinking it was my wife, I turned round. There was my mother standing by me, looking radiantly healthy. I gasped, "Mum!" All she said was, "Andrew, I'm happy where I am," and disappeared. To this day, my wife doesn't believe me, but I can assure you that I wasn't dreaming.
—Andrew S.

Five a.m. is supposed to be the most auspicious time to experience psychic awareness. Many Eastern yogis recommend that this is the best time to meditate.

8 DOUBLES
AND DOPPELGANGERS

PHANTOMS OF THE LIVING

When I was fifteen years old, my family and I emigrated to Ontario, Canada, where my father worked in the steel plant. Dad was very ill and sick in bed, when I went with my friends to the youth club. On the way home, I said, "Here comes Dad to meet us." There was no mistaking him—a miner, short, bandy-legged, with his flat cap on his head. I rushed towards him, wondering how he had recovered so quickly, but as I approached, he was gone.

When I got home, he was in a coma, and he died a few hours later. To this day, I believe that it was his departing spirit that came to me to say good-bye. I loved him so much and will never forget this experience that happened so long ago now.

—Mrs. Edith G. W.

The Society of Psychical Research, which has since Victorian times studied paranormal phenomena, were intrigued by these so called phantoms of the living. Today there are many studies being conducted by doctors of the reports from people who have claimed to have left their bodies during critical illness. I agree with your own conclusion: your father was able to say good-bye before he passed over.

I SAW MY OWN GHOST!

I believe that I am a bit psychic. I can literally "smell" death around a person who I believe is going to die. Although I find the exact scent impossible to describe, my intuition inevitably proves correct.

Very recently, I had a very peculiar experience. I was standing in front of the mirror. Suddenly, I felt as if someone else was in the room. I turned around and there, wearing totally different clothes, I saw myself with a big smile across my face! I was soon to go into hospital and at first thought the worst, but there was no "smell" of death. My operation was completely successful.

—Mrs. Jane D.

You saw your double, known as a *doppelganger*. These puzzling apparitions of the living are often seen at times of crisis. The famous German writer Goethe had a similar experience. He saw his own ghost walking along the road. Years later, at the same place, he saw his own ghost again, but the roles were reversed. Goethe realised that the first apparition was of him in the future, and the second was of him in the past. You saw yourself in the future, happy after your successful operation. The absence of the "smell" of death was an additional reassurance you that you'd be alright.

CELEBRITY GHOST LENDS A HAND

My American friend's car broke down one night. A man came and helped, and we recognised him as a famous celebrity. A few days later, we read in the paper that the celebrity had died in hospital at the exact time he had helped us to fix the car.
—George O.

You were probably helped by someone who was the spitting image of the celebrity. However, the timing makes this a very spooky coincidence.

I WAS IN TWO PLACES AT ONCE

A couple of weeks ago, I had a most strange experience. I got out of bed, and when I turned round, I saw myself still asleep, flat out in bed. There were two of me. I can't stop thinking about this very vivid experience.
—Ethel P.

Phantom appearances are not always of the dead. The effect you witnessed is known as the *doppelganger* or double. People have often reported seeing their double, usually performing mundane tasks and oblivious to the observer. Sometimes these spontaneous phantoms have been witnessed by groups of people. Elizabeth I is supposed to have had this experience in 1602, and one chronicler writes that she saw it lying on the bed, "pallid, shrivelled, and wan."

I'VE ONLY GOT ONE PAIR OF HANDS

One evening, my Mum said she was going to make a cup of tea. I could see her in the kitchen doing this, but I could also see her sitting reading, in

the same position in the living room, at the same time!

—A. D.

Reports of the *doppelganger*, or double, occur throughout history. Pope Alexander VI, Sir Gilbert Parker, and Queen Elizabeth I have all experienced this.

GRANDSON FRIGHTENED BY HIS DOUBLE

Last week my grandson (age fifteen) heard a noise from the shed and went to investigate. There he saw an image of himself. At first he saw half of his face and then, bit by bit, the whole face appeared.

He was very frightened by what he saw and ran into the house, telling his mother that he thought he was going to die. Since this day, he hasn't been well, and we fear for the worst.

—E. McK.

Studies of this phenomenon have shown that there is no correlation between seeing your double and a death. For example, as a young man, the famous German poet and writer Johann Goethe saw a ghost of himself pass him as he walked along the road. Years later, as an old man, he saw himself again at the same place, but this time as a young man and coming from the opposite direction.

9 ANIMAL ESP AND GHOSTS

THE FAIRY BRIDGE

In 1966 my wife and I decided to holiday on the Isle of Skye. It was an evening in August when we approached the bridge near Dunvegin. We came across an enormous number of cats. They were everywhere, and there were even some jumping on to the bonnet of our van. I said to my wife, "We are surely reaching civilisation, as there are plenty of cats around!" Later we stopped at the local inn and asked about the bridge. The landlord told us that it was nicknamed the Fairy Bridge and also known as the Bridge of Cats. He said that years ago, the bridge was the haunt of a witch, and that sometimes the place is haunted by the spirits of her cats!
—Ernest R.

Scottish folklore is filled with stories of spirit animals, sprites, and fairies. There's an extraordinary community that live on the Moray Firth called the Findhorn Foundation. They have nothing whatever to do with witchcraft, but do believe in the powers of positive nature spirits called *devas*. By harnessing these forces, they have transformed a barren area of land, without the aid of fertilisers, into one of the most lush and prolific places in Scotland.

IS MY DOG AWARE OF SPIRITS?

As I write, my dog is staring up at the front window. He has done this ever since my husband's brother died. Even on still nights, from the same window we hear knocking sounds. One morning we found a long row of pearls, in a perfect straight line, that had fallen from the nearby lightshade during the night. And on another occasion we witnessed a glass start tapping and move all by itself.
—Mrs Joan H.

Animals certainly appear to exhibit ESP and may be aware of spirit presence. Scientific tests have shown that many dogs respond when their owners make the decision to return home from an outing. I am not entirely convinced that the things you describe prove that your husband's brother is trying to make contact. There may yet be a simple reason for the knocking sounds and the glass shaking, such as traffic vibration, but the pearls laid neatly in a row takes some explaining.

MY FELINE FLOWER

My cat was dying of cancer of the liver and wouldn't come to bed, so I stayed up through the night nursing her. At 3:00 a.m., my attention was drawn to a large, pale pink hydrangea plant outside the living room window. As I watched, the flower changed to a vivid electric blue, even though the street lights were yellow. After a few minutes the

flower returned to normal and my little cat died in my arms.
—Iris B.

For some of us, pets are almost as important as people. When the flower changed colour, you were perhaps being shown that there is a place in the afterlife for all living things capable of love.

MY SHAME

As a young boy, I swapped my football and bag of sweets for a second-hand air-rifle. Eager to try out my new possession, I went into our back garden to find a suitable target. I am ashamed to say that I crept up on a mouse and shot it in the back of the neck. The slug didn't kill it, so I dropped it into a nearby bucket of water. The mouse began to spin like a top and then slowly sank to the bottom, motionless.

To my astonishment, although the mouse remained on the bottom of the bucket, I saw its identical form slowly rising to the surface and up into the sunlight, where it disappeared. I had not imagined this. What did I see?
—Charles C.

Of course, what you saw could have been a trick of the light caused by refraction. However, psychics believe that when a being dies, the spirit body continues. This "astral body" is a duplicate of the physical and is possessed by animals as well as humans. Nurses often report seeing this form leaving their dying patients. Your child's eyes were opened to a more spiritual way of being.

PUSSY CAT POLTERGEIST ROCKS HOME

Some time ago, my little tabby cat, Twinkle, had to be put to sleep. When she was alive, one of her favourite places to sleep was in the conservatory on a cushion on the end of the coffee table, near a wicker stand.

One warm, still June day, I saw the heavy wicker stand shake furiously I stood for what seemed ages—but must have in reality been a few minutes—and watched as the plants nearby rattled in their saucers. I could hardly believe my eyes, but will never forget what I saw.

What happened has never been explained to me. I've always had the feeling it was Twinkle. She was a very happy psychic cat when alive.

—Doreen J.

And I can't explain either. Maybe the shaking was caused by the wood of the wicker stand expanding in the heat. Or maybe a heavy lorry going by made your house tremor. Or just maybe it was the spirit of Twinkle letting you know she's all right.

DEAD HOWLER

One night, my dog began howling at 3:00 a.m. At first, I thought we may have a burglar, or perhaps there was a prowler about. Suddenly a small, round light flashed across the room and disappeared. The next morning at 11:00 a.m. I received a phone call to tell me that a close relative had died—at 3:00 a.m.!

—Judith F.

Animals are certainly psychic. Our little Jack Russell dog, William, will sense the presence of a spirit person in the house. Your dog seems to have the same ability.

The fact that he howled at 3:00 a.m. must either be an extraordinary coincidence, or there was a spirit presence in your room. Often when we see a spirit, it appears as a small light, as you have described. When a person first passes over to the spirit world, one of their first considerations is to reassure the living that they are alright. No doubt your relative tried to do just this.

DOGGY HEAVEN

I owned a dog who used to follow me everywhere. We had a very strong bond, and it seemed so unfair when he was killed in a road accident. I was wondering if there is a spirit world for animals? One evening, when I was feeling rather down, I was convinced that I felt my dog brush against my leg. Such a feeling of love came over me.
—Anna H.

Yes, there is an animal kingdom in the spirit world. That very special bond of love you have with your pet never stops. Often, when a loved one makes a communication through a medium, they bring with them and describe the pets that have passed over. Animals can't talk when they are here, and they don't suddenly start speaking when they get to the spirit. It normally takes a human spirit communicator to pass on their love. In your case, you're very lucky to be sensitive enough to feel the presence of your dog without the aid of a medium. No doubt your dog responded to your sadness and wanted to reassure you in the only way he knew how.

GHOST PATS THE DOG

I get very frightened by what seems to be a ghost that visits our house. One evening, I was sitting in our living room with my husband when I felt a cold, ghostly hand touch me. Our dog jumped up and seemed to be following something in the room. Then

he sat down and moved his head in such a way as to suggest that someone was petting his head.

I assure you that I am quite sane and don't have an over active imagination, but when these things happen, they frighten me so much. What should I do?
—Jill L.

Certainly, dogs and animals are very psychic. Maybe humans in the early stages of evolution were the same. It may have been part of our survival function to be able to distinguish intuitively between places that had a good atmosphere and those that were dangerous. Dogs seem to retain this ability and can even sense spirits.

However, it's important not to get jumpy or worried at every cold shudder we feel and assume that it's a malevolent presence. If what you describe does turn out to be real, it certainly couldn't hurt you. It's even been kind enough to take the trouble to pet the dog.

PENNY DIDN'T GO TO HEAVEN

Some months ago I read a copy of your book *The Psychic Handbook* that explains how ordinary people can develop ESP and healing abilities. When my cat, Penny, started suffering from fits, the vet said that she probably had brain damage and would definitely have to be put to sleep. I was so distressed that the vet suggested that he come back the next day.

Instead of giving up, I decided to consciously practice spiritual healing on her. I cradled her perspiration-soaked body in my arms and inwardly prayed that the "spirit vets" would come to my aid. I imagined healing light flowing from me to her and stayed up all night doing this.

Although Penny had had thirteen fits since her illness, by the morning she was completely better. When the vet called back to put her down, she ran to greet him and played with her ball to show off. My face was radiant. "Well I can't believe it!" exclaimed the vet.

—Elizabeth H.

I believe that everybody can channel healing light. I think you've proved my point.

IS TIGGER STILL WITH ME?

I used to own a cat called Tigger, whom I rescued from disaster, and who lived with me for eighteen years. When he died, I was heart-broken. Some nights I feel a weight upon the bed, as if Tigger were lying beside me, and when I look there is an imprint in the bed clothes where he used to lie. Although I do not see Tigger's spirit, I'm sure he's with me. What do you think?

—Gerald M.

Most psychics and mediums believe that all self-aware animals survive death. The bond of love between you and your pet is so great that nothing can separate you.

DOG'S JEALOUS GHOST GETS HIS OWN WAY

Our Corgi dog, Luke, used to be quite a rascal. He would always get his own way and was very spoiled. Sadly, in March this year he died of a kidney complaint. A week later we decided to buy a new puppy of the same breed. But the puppy is having an awful life because Luke, we believe, is tormenting him from the other side.

When he snuggles into Luke's favourite sleeping place, he yelps like he's being bitten and cowers against the wall. Before being fed, he waits in the same place as Luke did. It's as if he's being told to.

My wife keeps thinking that there are two dogs in the house. Finally, we had proof that Luke was up to his mischief. When we took a photo of our new puppy, there was a misty form behind him. It was the ghost of Luke!

—Jim W.

Dogs, like the wolves they were originally bred from, are pack animals. It is difficult to introduce a new dog into the pack (which includes, to Luke, you and your wife). Clearly, dogs must retain their instincts even beyond the grave.

MY KNOWING PETS

I am a pensioner living alone and have become very close to my dog, Penny, and cat, Kiri. Just like your other correspondents, I feel that my pets know exactly what I'm thinking. I'm sure that they respond to my thoughts. Perhaps, over a long period of time, they develop similar personalities to their owners because of our telepathic influence. I'm a gentle and placid person, and both my pets, since they were rescued from homes, have now developed a similar temperament to myself.

However, pets also respond to our routines. For example Penny always knows when I'm to take her with me to visit my friend, as I go the same time every week. Penny and Kiri also know when I'm to return home, as they sit in the window waiting for me.

To test whether they were sitting there the whole time I was away, on a number of occasions I've returned home to sneak a look. They weren't in the window. Only when I decided to return home early and go back in doors did they appear. On one occasion, I arrived at my normal time but stood outside in the street, talking to my friend for some

time. At the exact time I thought that I'd better go indoors, Kiri and Penny jumped up onto the window. Pets have an amazing sense of timing, but they could be psychic as well!
—Mrs P. M.

I'm sure that both animals and humans have an internal clock that helps us develop routines, such as getting up in the morning at the right time. It is interesting that your pets took no notice when you returned home with no intention of going indoors, but did react when you made a positive thought to enter your home.

BARKING MAD

My dog has a strange habit. He will suddenly leave the living room, dash upstairs to the bedroom, and start barking at the chair. It puzzled me for a long time until I had a consultation with a medium from the Christian Spiritualists. He made contact with my dead brother-in-law, Leslie, and said that he was saying, "Had we noticed the behaviour of our dog every time his spirit visited us and sat in the empty chair in the bedroom?"

Perhaps this explains my dog's strange behaviour?
—Mrs. Margaret P.

Assuming that you told the medium nothing about the dog's behaviour in advance, he may well be responding to a spirit presence.

Observing our dog, William, animals do appear to be aware when a spirit communication is taking place.

GHOST OF DOG BRINGS COMFORT

I loved my sheepdog, Mandy, and I was, of course, heart-broken when she died at Christmas. It took me a very long time to get over my grief. However, in May I saw something that lifted my heart and has since given me great comfort.

I was watching television and saw Mandy sitting in her usual place by the television.

What I saw was not a ghostly shape or an ephemeral shadow. What I saw was real. In fact, I got up from my chair and walked over to her. When I was just inches away from touching her with my fingers, she ran away and just disappeared into thin air.

I know that what I saw was not a trick of the imagination. It was a completely real experience. I believe that where there's love, there's no separation, and that Mandy is waiting for me to one day join her.

—Iris F.

It is my belief that at death animal souls merge into the collective soul of their species. However, animals that have experienced prolonged human love, such as pets, develop a sense of identity from their earthly experience. This self-awareness continues beyond death. Your love for Mandy has given her immortality.

DOGGED COINCIDENCE

Just before my mother died, my father told me of his vivid dream. In the dream, a black Labrador dog was tugging at his arm. When he awoke, he felt immersed in a deep peace. It was as if an immense silence fell over the house. Father told me that he believed that this was a sign that mother would die. We must prepare ourselves.

It is the custom to have a meal at home after a funeral. When the caterers arrived early in the morning to begin preparations, a black Labrador dog entered the house. We assumed it belonged with the caterers, but nobody knew whom the animal belonged to.

The dog immediately ran up the stairs and into the bedroom, in which Mother was laid out. "My goodness, it's the dog from my dream!" exclaimed Father.

After the funeral, we found an umbrella that someone had left behind. On the handle was a black Labrador's head. And for many days after, the same black Labrador dog continually sat in the road outside our house, looking up at mother's bedroom window.

—Frederick M.

In legends and mythology from around the world, dogs have guided the dead to the afterlife—a fitting symbol for your father's dream and series of coincidences. Dogs have traditionally been thought to possess the ability to see ghosts and "smell" death. It may well be that they are sensitive to chemical changes in human tissues, for there are many instances on record of dogs showing great distress hours before the death of their beloved master.

SPOOKY CAT WAS A SIGN

I was missing my late sister as I lay on my bed one afternoon. I looked at her photograph and said, "Please, please give me a sign to say that you're all right."

No sooner had I finished speaking, when I heard the sound of a cat. It was quite a loud call, so I got up and went to the window. I heard it meow again and turned around to see a black cat sitting on my bed!

"How on earth did you get in here?" I exclaimed in shock. But as I walked towards it to let it out, it just faded and disappeared in front of my eyes.

—Mrs. O. M.

It seems that you asked for a sign and got more than you bargained for The apparition of a cat was a symbolic reminder of your sister's love for these animals. Perhaps it was your subconscious or even your sister's spirit that was the source of this vision.

ALSATIAN DOG SENSED DISTRESS

A close friend of mine loved her Alsatian dog, who was put to sleep about a year before my friend died in November last year.

I was very distressed at my friend's funeral. Then an Alsatian dog entered the building and immediately made a tremendous fuss over me. He seemed not to want to leave me alone, and we decided to ring the owner, whose number was written on the tag on the dog's collar.

"This is the first time my dog has ever got out!" said the surprised owner. "And why on earth he should head for the chapel of rest, I really don't know." In fact, the warm memories that I associated with Alsatians and my friend brought me a great deal of comfort. Do you think that there's a hidden message to these events?
—Nan M.

It's probably just a coincidence that the dog headed for the chapel of rest. He must have also sensed your distress and wanted to comfort you. The fact that Alsatians reminded you of your departed friend is an added bonus. I believe that meaningful coincidences like this happen as a reflection of processes happening deep within our unconscious. The special message was to let you know your friend was happy in her new life.

HEALERS: BEWARE OF THE DOG

My dog is perfectly well-behaved at all times. But when a spiritual healer comes to visit me once a week to help me over my illness, the dog growls continually and keeps it up even after he's gone. Do you think he's psychic?
—Mrs K.

You pet may be seeing the invisible spirit helpers who may be working with your hearer friend. I'm convinced a great many pets are psychic. We are always interested to hear from readers with their psychic pet stories.

MY LITTLE PONY'S BROKEN HEART

When I was a child, my uncle owned a pony called Dolly, which he would dote on. He was unmarried and lived with his parents. Dolly was the only love in his life.

But my uncle became ill and was taken to Birmingham Hospital, where he died. He had been away for long periods before, and particularly during the war, but the look that was now in Dolly's eyes was of unmistakable sadness.

She knew that this time he wasn't coming back. From the moment he died, Dolly wouldn't eat or drink. "There was nothing I could do," confessed the vet when Dolly passed away. "She died of a broken heart."
—Mrs. E. C.

Your touching story illustrates that animals have feelings and are in inexplicable ways bound to us in love. From Dolly's behaviour, it appears that she "knew" that her master was dead. But how? She must have had extra sensory powers.

UPSET BY GHOST OF DOG

It was two weeks after my fourteen-year-old dog was put to sleep that I saw his spirit come through the window as I lay in bed reading. This upset me greatly, not because I was scared, but because I presumed that his spirit was at rest. Here he was, visiting me as a ghost. Was his soul not at peace?

—Mrs. C.

People wrongly assume that death is like an eternal sleep—we even carve "Rest in Peace" on gravestones. In reality, we awaken to a new world of even greater awareness than we know on earth and gain inner peace from knowing our eternal nature. And this applies to sentient animals as well.

10 QUESTIONS AND ANSWERS

WHAT CLOTHES DO SPIRITS WEAR?

When we die, we are wrapped in a shroud. However, when people describe seeing a ghost or apparition, they are clad in clothes that they wore in life. Is there an explanation for this?
—Len S.

When a spirit communicates with us, they show themselves as we knew them when they were alive. In the spirit world, they become beings of pure light. Children grow up as time passes, and the old become young again. We would not recognise them with our earthly eyes, so they show themselves in a form we can remember—including the clothes.

HOLLYWOOD GHOSTS

Do you think that the film *Ghost*, staring Patrick Swayze, Demi Moore, and Whoopi Goldberg, was a good representation of how mediums and psychics envisage the other side of life, or was it just another

Hollywood fantasy? I drew a lot of comfort from the film and would like to think that it contains some truth.
—Mrs. Susan B.

Ghost has been acclaimed by many leading psychics as being one of the most well-researched and accurate films about spirit communication. Prior to making the film, Patrick Swayze visited many of the organizations dedicated to psychical research and mediumship. We met Patrick Swayze on the set of our show on *The Big Breakfast* and found him to be a very sincere and modest man. Apparently he also believes in the healing power of crystals and carries an amethyst in his pocket.

WE'LL MEET AGAIN—NO THANKS

I never got on with my wife when she was here, and I certainly don't want to meet up with her again after I die. What do you have to say about this?
—Colin B.

When you go down that tunnel of light, your wife certainly won't be waiting at the other end in her curlers and holding a rolling pin. In the spirit world, there are no jealousies or resentment. Like attracts like, and if we really don't get on with someone here, we won't be drawn together over there.

WORRIED BY GHOST ADVICE

I always read your column with great interest but feel that you've neglected to say something of great importance when writing about ghostly occurrences. Are not these spirits stuck on the earth plane by their very strong attachments to this world here?

I always feel that people who are troubled by these spirits should say to them, "Be at peace, blessings on you, and now continue on your path and leave the past behind."

It worries me that you do not advise this. Am I wrong in thinking this?

—Joan F.

You are absolutely right, of course. Earth-bound spirits are those that cling to the earth plane—usually because of fear or unresolved difficulties at the time of their passing. If anyone is troubled by "ghosts," send them thoughts of encouragement to continue on their path into the blissful realms of the afterlife. Help them with your loving thoughts to let go of this world.

HEAVENLY MESSENGER

Would it be possible to "pass" a message on to my grandparents, Irene and Hugh?

I would just like them to know that I have settled down in my career and made a name for myself. Also I want to apologise to them for all the pain and grief that I have caused to both them and my parents over the years. Please tell them that, even though I've had problems showing my feelings, I love them very much and miss them. I owe them so much for everything they did for me over the years.

—Charlie D.

Your grandparents know exactly what has been happening in your life and are well aware of your thoughts asking for forgiveness. They will sense your sincere and loving thoughts, and we're sure that they extend the same feelings back to you. The power of love knows no barrier. It can cross even the bridge between life and death. If you open your heart to them, you may feel their love around you.

WHAT HAPPENED TO MY BABY?

I had an abortion twelve years ago and have suffered guilt ever since. My parents have both passed on. What happens to babies and terminated foetuses? Do they go to the spirit world?
—Alison R.

Every soul is very precious and, yes, even terminated babies go back to the spirit world. Your child would have grown now, in spirit, and become more aware. Remember that your mother and father would have cared for your baby over there, and they would all understand your reasons for having a pregnancy termination. You are still that baby's earthly mother, and the love between you will continue to grow.

MY MOTHER'S GHOST SCARES ME

Ever since my mother died nine years ago, I have been frightened that her ghost will appear in front of me. If I awake in the night, I am terrified that I will see her. This has led to awful nightmares, and my husband is very worried about me. I loved my mother very much, but she died so suddenly that we didn't get a chance to say good-bye.
—Jean F.

Your fear of seeing your mothers spirit is partly due to the fact that you still haven't come to terms with her passing. We feel sure that your mother will not show herself to you if you don't want her to.

WHERE SHOULD I LOOK?

I have been interested in psychic phenomena for years and would like to meet a reliable psychic or medium. Could you advise me how I can arrange a sitting with a genuine practitioner?
—Mr. Terry A.

Your local paper's classified columns will contain many people advertising their services as clairvoyants and mediums, but in our experience few of these people have a genuine psychic gift. The best psychics tend not to advertise, as they are usually in great demand.

I suggest you write or email the Arthur Findlay College, Stanstead Hall, Stanstead Mountfitchet, Essex CM24 8UD. They will be able to advise you of trustworthy mediums working in your area.

You can also contact mediums through my website and the numbers listed at the end of the book.

SUICIDE WORRY

Can you give any information about, or do you have any knowledge of, the belief that people who commit suicide never rest when they reach "the other side." I am a religious person, and this is important to me.
—Sarah B.

I have made many mediumistic communications for people who have lost loved ones through suicide. The spirit communicators explain that when they enter the spirit, they are helped to come to terms with their problems by advanced spiritual helpers. At first they are restless, as there are still problems to be resolved, but this is not a permanent condition. Through the power of love they are helped to become at peace with themselves. If you have lost someone yourself through suicide, send them loving thoughts, as this will help them.

I WANT TO GIVE MY BODY TO SCIENCE

When I die, I want to donate my organs to medicine so that others may live. I believe in life after death and of the possibility of reincarnation, but I am concerned that if I become a donor when I go to the Spirit, I will not be whole. Please could you ease my mind about this dilemma.
—Anne B.

The spirit body is independent of the physical body. It doesn't matter what happens to our physical body after we are gone. Whether it is buried, cremated, or left to science, it is no longer our concern once we are in Spirit.

What matters is the level of spirituality that we develop in this life. This is the treasure that worm and moth cannot corrupt.

DO ANIMALS SURVIVE DEATH?

Could you please let me know if you know for certain whether animals have souls, and if they reach the next world? Please let me know, as it means a lot to me.
—Wanda P.

An advanced North American Indian spirit teacher named Silver Birch spoke a great deal about the survival of animals through the mouthpiece of his medium, Hannen Swaffer. Most mediums, including myself, accept that pets and well-loved animals survive death. Silver Birch taught that an animal survives because their soul spiritually develops through contact with humans. Wild animals join the collective soul of their species.

IS HEAVEN CROWDED?

Although there were been several fraudulent mediums exposed earlier this century, I am convinced that psychic communication is now a proven fact. There is just so much documented evidence to support this. However, where do all these spirits go? If all human, and perhaps animal, spirits have survived since the Stone Age, then heaven must be very overcrowded. I think the Hindus have it right. We reincarnate over many lives, and the number of spirits is therefore limited. What do you think?
—Harry H. A.

I believe that in the afterlife there are worlds beyond worlds. The human spirit continues to evolve into eve higher spiritual planes, which exist outside space and time. There is an eternal progress that is open to every sentient being. However, I also believe that, at the early stages of the soul's evolution, we reincarnate. We spend some time in the afterlife then return here to learn more from earthly life.

DOES HE HATE ME?

I split up with my ex-husband seven years ago because he had a drink problem. Eventually I met someone else, and my divorce came through. He disappeared soon after this, and about a year later they found his skeleton in a bushy area of a field. I have tried to make contact with him through spiritualists and psychics but to no avail. Do you think that he hates me?
—Mary Y.

Don't blame yourself. Drink can do terrible things to people and was the root cause of his death. Once in the spirit world, your ex would have been cared for in the healing halls to bring him face to face with his actions in life. It would take some time before he is whole again. Just because you have had no spirit contact from him doesn't mean that he hates you.

DO MUM AND DAD KNOW ABOUT THE BABY?

I lost both my parents three years ago. Since then I have given birth to a baby daughter. Do you think that there is any way that they could know that she has been born?
—Jacqueline F.

Of course Mum and Dad know about the birth—they probably witnessed it from the Spirit. Although only a few of us can see the spirit people, it is easy for them to see us.

X MARKS THE SPOT

Sometimes I can feel the presence of my deceased mother near me. One night I saw, in the middle of the room, a figure. I knew it was human, but it was as if it was standing behind a Perspex corrugated sheet. Another thing that bothers me a little is that I feel as if someone presses, with their thumbnail, the sign of the cross onto my forehead. I am very interested in life after death, but am I imagining these things?
—John R.

You have the beginnings of a mediumistic ability, but there are still barriers to be dismantled. The spirit figure showed you this. The centre of the forehead is where clairvoyance is focused. Some clairvoyants visualise this psychic centre as a cross within an indigo light, and yours is starting to open.

BANISH GRIEF

My husband does not believe in an afterlife and refuses to let me visit a medium. Five years ago, we lost our son, and I am worried that he may be trying to reach us but is unable to do so.

I cannot bear the thought that he is trying to reach us and thinks we have forgotten him. My husband says this will not be happening, but I cannot stop worrying about it.

—A worried mother

Your son is not in distress because he cannot find a channel to communicate with you. He can see you and will know your thoughts. Send him thoughts of love that help him with his spiritual progress, and banish the thoughts of grief.

DID THE GREAT HOUDINI ESCAPE DEATH?

Has anyone succeeded in deciphering the coded message the Great Houdini left after his death? He was perhaps also one of the greatest debunkers of ghosts and spirits.

According to the journalist Maurice Barbanell, Houdini's wife, Bess, in the presence of Walter Winchell, the famous American columnist, signed a sworn affidavit that a coded message arranged between herself and Houdini, in its exact form, was received through the mediumship of Arthur Ford.

I understand that later, after much adverse criticism, she retracted her statement. Is it possible to settle the argument?

—James T.

On Halloween 1926, Houdini died of peritonitis, and his widow, Bess, was besieged by dozens of mediums, all claiming to be in contact with her dead husband. On January 8, 1929, she sat with the trance medium Arthur Ford, who gave the strange message, "Rosabelle, answer, tell, pray, answer, look, tell, answer, answer, tell."

Engraved inside the wedding ring of Bess was the song "Rosabelle, sweet Rosabelle, / I love you more than I can tell. / Over me you cast a spell / I love you, my sweet Rosabelle." This song dated back to the earliest days of the Houdini act and was the numbered word-code used in his mind-reading act. When decoded, the spirit message consisted of just one word: *Believe.*

However Joseph Dunninger, the master radio mentalist, pointed out that the message could be a fraud. The secret code had been published in Houdini's biography just one year after the magician's death. Bess reluctantly withdrew her sponsorship of Arthur Ford's communication.

Bess, however, continued to believe that her husband had attempted to communicate with her and also continued to sit with mediums hoping for a true message. Apparently there was an authentic message, but the secret died with her when she passed in 1948. Just before she died, she told a friend: "When I go, I'll be gone for good. I won't even try to come back."

MY EVIL EYES

I have one blue eye and one brown one. I used to be taunted at school because of this. I read that in the sixteenth century people like me were thought to have the "evil eye" and were burned as witches—so perhaps things could have been worse. Some also say that with my eyes, I should be able to see ghosts and

spirits. I don't believe that I have any special powers. What do you think about this?
—Marie F.

The same superstition also applied to people with eyes set close together or deep in their head. In the Far East, however, the superstition is quite the opposite. A Buddhist monk in Thailand is currently asking $4 million for his white Siamese cat, which has one brilliant blue eye. So next time people get catty, remind them of your exalted Eastern counterpart.

IT'S WRITTEN ALL OVER THEIR FACE

Sometimes I can look at a young person, and I see their face change. I see the face of what they will look like when old superimposed over their own face, like a translucent mask. I wonder sometimes if I am seeing spirits over the person's face. This doesn't happen with everyone. What do you think I am seeing? I would love an explanation.
—J. M.

I've seen this myself and have puzzled over what it for some time. My conclusion is that we see, not the future, but the faces of a person's past incarnations. Many years ago, I took part in a series of intriguing reincarnation experiments in Holland, in which we were separated into pairs and had to gaze at each other's faces for half an hour without speaking. It was a very strange experience, particularly as I'd never met the person I was sitting with before. Afterwards we all compared notes and realised that many of us were communicating by thought and, in addition, had seen strange faces from many different cultures superimposed upon each other's features.

HOW CAN I TELL IF IT'S TRUE?

For a long time I did automatic writing. The pen in my hand would take on a life of its own and, although I was holding it, write messages from friends who had passed to Spirit. Facts were given about the person's life that I had no knowledge of, and which had to be checked afterwards.

But what started off so wonderfully has now deteriorated into nonsense. Some of the first messages, I'm sure, were true, but now my pen reads the thoughts of people in the room.

I'm now finding it hard to distinguish between what is spirit communication and what is telepathy.

—Mrs. Marjorie H.

All forms of mediumship can be influenced by the thoughts of the people around you. As your powers increase—and with experience—you will learn to distinguish between what is telepathy and what is not. Do not be afraid to admit to the people that sit with you that telepathy can interfere. They will realise that you are sincere. Use your common sense to discriminate between fact and falsehood.

AGONY OVER SON'S SUICIDE

Just before Christmas last year, my son, Peter, committed suicide by shooting himself. I lost touch with my son six years ago, after I fell out with his wife. They didn't even get in touch when I was taken into hospital with a serious cancer operation.

I feel so hurt and sometimes angry. Peter left no suicide note to his wife, his three daughters, or myself. I can't bear to think what he was going through before his death. Has he now found peace?

—Mrs. Q. H.

Mediums believe that after a person takes their own life they are taken to a part of the spirit world called "The Halls of Healing." Here they are helped by the higher spiritual beings to come to terms with what they have done. The pain, guilt, and anguish that they felt as they made their transition is gradually resolved. Your son is now be basking in the peace that permeates the afterlife.

.

MORE BOOKS BY CRAIG

Hamilton-Parker, Craig & Jane (1995). *The Psychic Workbook*. Random House. ISBN 0-09-179086-7 (Languages: English, Chinese).

Hamilton-Parker, Craig (1996). *Your Psychic Powers*. Hodder & Stoughton. ISBN 0-340-67417-2 (Languages: English)

Hamilton-Parker, Craig (1999). *Timeless Wisdom of the Tibetans*. Hodder & Stoughton. ISBN 0-340-70483-7 (Languages: English)

Hamilton-Parker, Craig (1999). *The Psychic Casebook*. Blandford/Sterling. ISBN 0-7137-2755-1 (Languages: English, Turkish).

Hamilton-Parker, Craig (1999). *The Hidden Meaning of Dreams*. Sterling imprint, Barnes & Noble. ISBN 0-8069-7773-6 (Languages: English, Spanish, Portuguese, Russian, Israeli, Greek, Icelandic).

Hamilton-Parker, Craig (2000). *The Intuition Pack*. Godfield Books. ISBN 1-84181-007-X.

Hamilton-Parker, Craig (2000). *Remembering Your Dreams*. Sterling imprint, Barnes & Noble. ISBN 0-8069-4343-2.

Hamilton-Parker, Craig (2000). *Unlock Your Secret Dreams*. Sterling imprint, Barnes & Noble. ISBN 1-4027-0316-3.

Hamilton-Parker, Craig (2002). *Fantasy Dreaming*. Sterling imprint, Barnes & Noble. ISBN 0-8069-5478-7.

Hamilton-Parker, Craig (2003). *Protecting the Soul.* Sterling imprint, Barnes & Noble. ISBN 0-8069-8719-7.

Hamilton-Parker, Craig (2004). *Psychic Dreaming.* Sterling imprint, Barnes & Noble. ISBN 1-4027-0474-7

Hamilton-Parker, Craig (2005). *Opening to the Other Side.* Sterling imprint, Barnes & Noble. ISBN 1-4027-1346-0.

Hamilton-Parker, Craig (2010). *What To Do When You Are Dead.* Sterling imprint, Barnes & Noble. ISBN 978-1-4027-7660-1 (Languages: English, Dutch, Portuguese).

Hamilton-Parker, Craig with Kipling, Violet (2014). *Psychics & Mediums Network Training Manuals.* Amazon.com. ISBN 1503126048.

Hamilton-Parker, Craig (2014). *The Dream Handbook.* Amazon.com. ISBN 1503004309.

Hamilton-Parker, Craig (2014). *Psychic Protection.* Amazon.com. ISBN 1501005642.

Hamilton-Parker, Craig (2014). *A Medium's Guide to Psychic Dream Interpretation.* Amazon.com. ISBN 1500924474.

Hamilton-Parker, Craig (2014). *Psychic School.* Amazon.com. ISBN 150247798X

Hamilton-Parker, Craig (2014). *Psychic Encounters.* Amazon.com. ISBN 1500759228.

Hamilton-Parker, Craig (2014). *Tibetan Buddhism in Daily Life.* Amazon.com. ISBN 1502554933.

Hamilton-Parker, Craig (2014). *Your Psychic Powers.* Amazon.com. ISBN 1500807230.

Hamilton-Parker, Craig (2014). *Common Dream Meanings.* Amazon.com. ISBN 1502775778.

Hamilton-Parker, Craig (2014). *Phantoms on Film.* Amazon.com. ISBN 1507646687.

Hamilton-Parker, Craig (2014). *Real Angels & Spiritual Encounters.* Amazon.com. ISBN 1505611547.

YOU MAY ALSO ENJOY

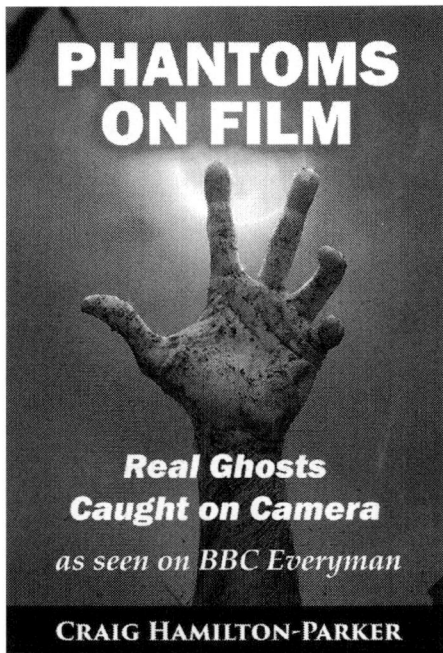

PHANTOMS ON FILM
By Craig Hamilton-Parker

Phantoms on Film **is an intriguing collection of real ghost photographs and paranormal phenomena captured on camera.**
With 40 years' experience as a medium communicating with the dead, Craig is hailed by the media as the world's leading expert on paranormal image analysis. Craig uses his skills to sort out the phantoms from the fakes

Available from: psychics.co.uk

YOU MAY ALSO ENJOY

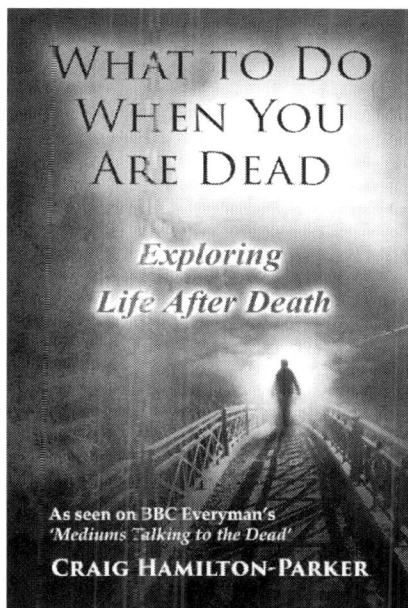

WHAT TO DO WHEN YOU ARE DEAD
By Craig Hamilton-Parker

Is there life after death? Author and Spiritualist medium Craig Hamilton-Parker draws on cross cultural beliefs and his own work to describe what life in the afterlife is like.

This book will help you to overcome the fear of death and prepare you for the next-life. Based on extensive research and direct insights the book builds a picture of what the afterlife is like and what life is like on the other side.

Available from: psychics.co.uk

YOU MAY ALSO ENJOY

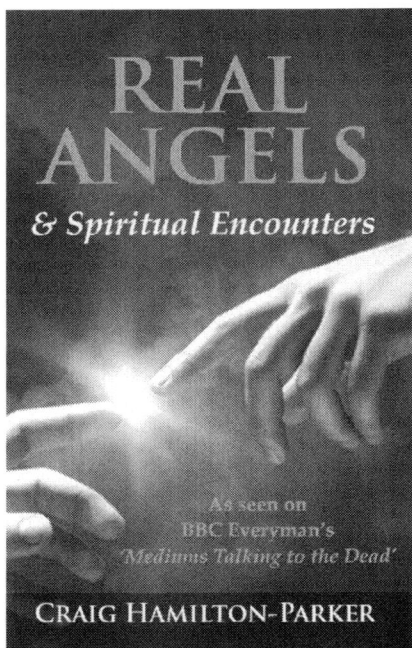

ONLINE PSYCHIC SCHOOL

At our Online Psychic School, we have classes, courses, and circles happening most weekdays, as well as a thriving community of spiritually minded people.

Join our Online Psychic School:
psychics.co.uk

CLAIRVOYANCE SERVICES

Craig and Jane Hamilton-Parker offer psychic and mediumistic readings from their website. They also have an online community, where you can ask questions and share your paranormal dreams and psychic insights with like-minded people.

Visit: psychics.co.uk

If you would like a reading today, you can call their telephone psychics and book a reading on the numbers below:

UK: **0800 067 8600**
USA: **1-855-444-6887**
EIRE: **1 800 719 656**
AUSTRALIA: 1800 825 305

Callers must be 18 or over to use this service and have the bill payers permission. For entertainment purposes only. All calls are recorded PhonePayPlus regulated SP: StreamLive Ltd, EC4R 1BB, 0800 0673 330.

ABOUT THE AUTHOR

Craig Hamilton-Parker is a British author, television personality, and professional psychic medium. He is best known for his television shows *Our Psychic Family*, *The Spirit of Diana*, and *Nightmares Decoded*. On television, he usually works with his wife **Jane Hamilton-Parker**, who is also a psychic medium. Their work was showcased in a three-part documentary on the BBC called *Mediums Talking to the Dead*.

They now have TV shows in the U.S.A. and spend a lot of time demonstrating mediumship around the world.

Born in Southampton, UK, Craig was convinced at an early age that he was mediumistic. He became well-known as a platform medium within Spiritualism and in 1994 left his job as an advertising executive to become the resident psychic on Channel 4 television's *The Big Breakfast*, making predictions for upcoming news stories. He wrote a regular psychic advice column for *The Scottish Daily Record* and regular features for *The Daily Mail*, *Sunday Mirror*, and *The People*.

His first book in the psychic genre was published in 1995, and his books are now finding a world audience and are published in many languages.

You can find out more and join Craig and Jane's work and Spiritual Foundation at their website, **psychics.co.uk**

23001976R00065

Printed in Great Britain
by Amazon